Language and culture
in British business

Also available from CILT, the National Centre for Languages:

Adults learning languages: A CILT guide to good practice
Edited by Henriette Harnisch and Pauline Swanton

European Language Portfolio for Adult and Vocational Purposes

Language learning for work in a multilingual world
Edited by Cherry Sewell

CILT, the National Centre for Languages, seeks to support and develop multilingualism and intercultural competence among all sectors of the population in the UK.

CILT serves education, business and the wider community with:
• specialised and impartial information services;
• high quality advice and professional development;
• expert support for innovation and development;
• quality improvement in language skills and service provision.

CILT is a charitable trust, supported by the DfES and other Government departments throughout the UK.

Language and culture in British business

Communication, needs and strategies

Stephen Hagen

The views expressed in this publication are the author's and do not necessarily represent those of CILT.

First published 2005
by CILT, the National Centre for Languages
20 Bedfordbury
London
WC2N 4LB

Copyright © CILT, the National Centre for Languages 2005

Front cover photography: Getty Images and Corel Corporation

ISBN 1 904243 33 9

A catalogue record for this book is available from the British Library.

Printed in Great Britain by Hobbs

CILT Publications are available from: **Central Books**, 99 Wallis Rd, London E9 5LN. Tel: 0845 458 9910. Fax: 0845 458 9912. Book trade representation (UK and Ireland): **Broadcast Book Services**, Charter House, 29a London Rd, Croydon CR0 2RE. Tel: 020 8681 8949. Fax: 020 8688 0615.

contents

Acknowledgements

This book could not have been completed without the assistance of several teams. Firstly, the all-important LNTO Language skills capacity audits for England and Wales were ably and successfully managed by the LNTO team, led by Derek Winslow, previous CEO, comprising Dr Anne Davidson Lund and Dominic Luddy, who were also responsible for collating the provision-side statistics. Secondly, particular thanks go to the team at InterAct International, namely, Helena Christie, Stuart Williams and Lisa Willoughby, who managed most of the demand-side surveys for the LNTO/CILT Language skills capacity audits and collated the aggregated datasets for this publication. I am grateful to Helena Christie, Stuart Williams and Lisa Willoughby for their support, critical reading, insightful comments and supreme understanding in the time-consuming preparation of the final version.

I am also grateful to support from the INTERCOMM and PROTOCOL 12 projects of the EU's Leonardo da Vinci Programme for informing work in Chapters 3 and 4 respectively. Furthermore, the European data was collated thanks to support from the REFLECT project of the Leonardo da Vinci Programme.

This book is dedicated to Susanne Hagen for making her own cross-border commitment to life in England.

preface

This book collates and analyses data from the most recent quantitative and qualitative surveys of business language and culture in UK trade and commerce. The most comprehensive of these are the seven LNTO/CILT Language skills capacity audits (known collectively as the LNTO/CILT language skills audits) undertaken by the Languages National Training Organisation (LNTO)/CILT, the National Centre for Languages, between 2000 and 2003.

Parallel methodology was used to conduct all seven LNTO/CILT language skills audits, covering six English regions (East, North East, North West, South West, West Midlands, Yorkshire and the Humber) and Wales. The data from the Welsh and the six English surveys has been aggregated to form a single percentage for England and Wales. The survey findings are presented in accessible tables, graphs and charts, as appropriate. Full versions of the seven audits are also available on the CILT website (**www.cilt.org.uk**). All the studies introduce qualitative work which is included in the form of case studies of export companies designed to illustrate different approaches to trading abroad as well as providing insights into the nature of language barriers which many UK exporters face today.

Observations on methodology

While the seven LNTO/CILT language skills audits do not collectively represent a truly national picture, since the key regions of London and the South East are absent, they do nonetheless give a valuable overview into the needs of British companies across most of the country. A recent small-scale feasibility study was carried out in the South East of England in 2001. A major survey to be carried out in the capital is currently being discussed with key London development organisations.

The methodology applied in each of the language skills audits was based on self-reporting and self-selection and collated by means of a postal questionnaire. The survey populations were selected on the basis of their international trading profile and number of employees (up to 500 employees; data on trading activity in native English speaking countries was excluded). The same questionnaire was mailed in all areas, and was completed and returned by a total of 2,292 companies: 1,965 in six English regions and 327 in Wales (see Figure 1).

Data subsets for Scotland, Northern Ireland and the Republic of Ireland have been collated from two European surveys, **REFLECT** and **ELISE**, which use comparable methodology. Of these, the REFLECT project, financed in part by the EU Leonardo da Vinci Programme, involved a study of nearly 1,000 international small to medium-sized enterprises (SMEs) in four countries: Ireland, Poland, Portugal and the UK (see also Hagen and Salomao, 2003).

The samples in Figure 1 below do not give an exact statistical representation of the international companies in the region/country surveyed. The findings of the LNTO/CILT language skills audits are best interpreted as providing generalised tendencies for international companies using languages for trade in those regions.

Figure 1: Surveys and sample sizes

Country/region	Year of survey*	Sample size
East of England	LNTO/CILT(2003)	329
Wales	LNTO/CILT(2002)	327
North West of England	LNTO/CILT(2002)	303
West Midlands	LNTO/CILT(2001)	222
South West of England	LNTO/CILT(2001)	484
Yorkshire and Humber	LNTO/CILT(2001)	328
North East of England	LNTO/CILT(2000)	299
Ireland	REFLECT (2001)	233
Poland	REFLECT (2001)	166
Portugal	REFLECT (2001)	213
Denmark	ELISE (1999/2000)	52
Netherlands	ELISE (1999/2000)	92
Northern Ireland	ELISE (1999/2000)	50
Scotland	ELISE (1999/2000)	139
Sweden	ELISE (1999/2000)	44
France (Central)	ELUCIDATE (1996)	245
Germany (Southern)	ELUCIDATE (1996)	171
Spain (Western)	ELUCIDATE (1996)	124

* For year of publication, see References section

Notwithstanding its methodological and geographical limitations, the combined dataset offers the most comprehensive picture of business language use and need in European commerce and industry in the latter part of the twentieth and the early part of the twenty-first century. The REFLECT surveys were carried out in Europe in 2001 and 2002 and were designed to investigate and measure the impact of language and cultural barriers on European companies with up to 500 employees engaged in international trade, with particular reference to Ireland, Poland, Portugal and England (see Appendix 1 for further detail).

Thanks to the consistency of survey methodology, it has also been possible to draw longitudinal comparisons with *Business communication across borders: A study of language use and practice in European companies* (Hagen 1999); also known as the ELUCIDATE study, which was carried out in the mid-nineties thanks to a grant from the EU Leonardo da Vinci Programme.

Other national surveys reported in the study

The two other sources of data referred to extensively are the surveys conducted by Metra Martech (1999), commissioned for DTI and, more recently, the *British Chambers of Commerce language survey*, *The impact of foreign languages on British business*, which appears in two parts: Part 1: Qualitative (2003); Part 2: Quantitative (2004).

Country/region	Year of survey	Sample size
UK Regions	Metra Martech (1999 and 1997)	503
England	British Chambers of Commerce (2004)	1,038

The two Metra Martech language studies (1999 and 1997) and *British Chambers of Commerce language survey* (2004) use different methodology, which complements the LNTO/CILT language skills audits. The DTI's most recent Metra Martech language study (1999) reviewed patterns of language use and need in a sample of 503 UK export companies of diverse sizes (up to and beyond 500 employees) with a wide geographical spread across the UK and measured the changes that had occurred since 1997.

In the *British Chambers of Commerce language survey* the sample of 1,038 was segmented by the number of employees, and a quota was placed on each segment to ensure that a good cross-section of exporters was interviewed. For the purposes of analysis the sample was weighted to ensure it was proportionally representative of companies in England based on data held by Dun & Bradstreet, restricted to companies with up to 250 people.

The British Chambers of Commerce were primarily interested in investigating the link between language competence and export performance for export managers. The first report, launched in October 2003, documented the findings from a qualitative study involving a series of in-depth interviews with senior export executives. The objective of the qualitative research was to identify and segment the different behaviours and attitudes held by exporters in relation to trading in overseas markets and profile them for their motivations, ambitions, education and language competence.

The second part of the British Chambers of Commerce report was conducted in 2004 and involved 1,038 telephone interviews with business exporters of various sizes across England, in order to provide quantifiable results.

Qualitative work

Balancing the over-emphasis on the quantitative side, this publication also includes a series of the surveys' case studies of, interviews with, and quotations from, companies, export managers and so-called 'Influencers'. The latter are people with local business knowledge and influence, such as Chamber CEOs and International Trade Directors, whose views are critical to understanding the current climate for international traders and who can ultimately influence the course of action that companies, regional authorities and language suppliers are taking with regard to language policy, provision and trade.

introduction

The existence of a significant range of studies conducted not only within the UK but also across many parts of Europe over the last five years gives us a fascinating and unique insight into foreign language use, as well as the impact of communication barriers on the UK's overseas trade. They also provide possible strategic direction for policy-makers in central and local government and the development authorities by suggesting future patterns of language demand. Taken together, the findings offer a snapshot of how the average UK export company is performing in non-English speaking markets today. From this a number of solutions and recommendations arise on how companies can successfully face the prospect of trading in an ever-increasing global marketplace with its multitude of languages and cultures.

Aims of this book

The main aims of this book are to collate and, wherever the methodology permits, compare existing findings in order to draw out important generalisations about the use of languages in international trade. This applies to the LNTO/CILT language skills audits and various associated European surveys findings, where datasets can be compared and even merged, providing a wealth of insights and findings.

The LNTO/CILT language skills audits data broadly break down into six macro-categories of information:

- numbers of companies with linguistic expertise;
- levels of existing language skills of employees in enterprise;
- levels of language and/or cultural training being undertaken;
- types of language training undertaken;
- barriers to trade caused by lack of specific language/cultural skills;

- impact of language/cultural barriers on trade performance;
- international communication strategies employed, if any, to overcome these problems;
- use of translation agencies;
- likely future demand for communication skills (by target market).

The main findings referred to in this book are summarised in Figure 2 opposite. An average of the percentages for each region provides a broad overview of the situation in England and Wales (See column 9: 'Average of England and Wales'). Data for Northern Ireland and Scotland from the ELISE (2001) study has been included to offer comparisons where possible, though in both these cases the number of respondents is low by comparison with the English regions.

From the table it is possible to see where there are consistent patterns emerging in various regions or national administrations. It is also apparent that the small sample of Northern Ireland companies has produced some anomalies. The variance from the average for England and Wales (column 9) indicates that some regions seem to face greater problems; the East of England, for example, is above average for language and cultural barriers and has experienced higher levels of lost business than others. However, the more consistent the pattern across the subsets, the greater the likely accuracy of the local finding. For example, the percentage of companies experiencing cultural barriers is consistently one in five across all subsets. This suggests evidence of a national pattern.

Each chapter of the book reviews one key aspect of these findings in great detail, both quantitatively and qualitatively, i.e. 'Use of languages' (Chapter 1); 'Language barriers' (Chapter 2); 'Cultural barriers' (Chapter 3); 'Communication strategies' (Chapter 4); and 'Recommendations for action' (Chapter 5).

Figure 2: Summary of main findings

	North East (n=299)	Yorkshire and the Humber (n=328)	West Midlands (n=222)	South West (n=484)	Wales (n=327)	North West (n=303)	East (n=329)	Average of England & Wales	Northern Ireland (n=50)	Scotland (n=139)
Companies using at least one foreign language	60%	52%	70%	60%	53%	60%	60%	59%	52%	54%
Companies with at least one employee claiming foreign language*	62%	63%	67%	67%	63%	63%	74%	66%	42%	58%
Have experienced language barriers	46%	41%	50%	45%	42%	51%	47%	46%	38%	50%
Have lost business as a consequence	19%	20%	22%	20%	19%	22%	25%	21%	14%	6%
Have experienced cultural barriers	20%	20%	16%	23%	20%	20%	21%	20%	24%	17%
Have a language strategy	N/A	9%	14%	9%	9%	11%	11%	11%	12%	5%
Have invested in language training	22%	23%	25%	21%	22%	23%	27%	23%	8%	22%
Need language training in future	39%	33%	37%	34%	42%	38%	36%	37%	12%	38%
Anticipate trading in future in other countries	53%	47%	35%	36%	39%	44%	44%	43%	44%	46%
Use translators/interpreters	43%	52%	48%	48%	50%	58%	56%	51%	N/A	N/A

* In addition to English/Welsh

Main points arising

Which languages are most in use in UK business?

On average over half of the UK's exporting companies claim to use at least one foreign language in their international trade regularly. However, linguistic proficiency in UK companies falls short of the proficiency in companies in non-native English speaking parts of Europe. For example, 94% of Danish companies, 88% of Dutch companies and 89% of Swedish companies surveyed in ELUCIDATE claim to use at least one foreign language regularly.

Of companies in England and Wales, 53% declare that their language skills are only at basic or intermediate level. This is generally a consequence of the low standard of language skills among local employees, many of whom traditionally leave school with just a GCSE in French, or, rarely, German.

This picture is further confirmed from the findings of the British Chambers of Commerce language survey (2004) in which 80% of English export managers surveyed cannot competently conduct business dealings overseas in even one foreign language. It is also apparent from the LNTO/CILT language skills audits and DTI's Metra Martech study (1999) that language knowledge, particularly in SMEs, is concentrated mainly in managers and Managing Directors, while key staff at the interface with clients and customers, actual and potential (switchboard and reception staff, etc) are far less proficient, if at all.

Generally, proficiency is poor in the UK where spontaneity is required, e.g. answering the telephone, at meetings, socialising or travelling, and instructing foreign workers. This leads many UK companies (i.e. particularly those termed **Anglocentrics** and **Opportunists** by British Chambers of Commerce, 2003) to a heavy reliance on English for exporting. Often local agents overseas are chosen on the basis of their language rather than business acumen.

Common statements like 'we tend to rely on the English of our customers' do not, however, always bode ill for the British exporting effort, as English works work well in Scandinavia and regions of the former Commonwealth. But it is apparent that English is less widely understood in countries like Russia, China, Japan, as well as many parts of central and Eastern Europe. Nevertheless in the East of England, a fairly typical example, 40% of companies in the sample rely on English, or the intermediation of English-speaking agents, to do all their business. At the same time all the studies throw up examples of why not to rely on just English and particularly throw doubts on the wisom of employing local agents whose main qualification for the job is English.

Not surprisingly, French and German have consistently been the most widely used languages across all of UK business over many years (see Chapter 2). French comes out as the most widely used foreign language for British companies, followed closely by German. This is demonstrated by the LNTO/CILT language skills audits and Metra Martech (1997 and 1999). However, there are some significant variations for different parts of the UK. In Scotland and the North East of England, the difference between numbers of companies using French and German is only 1%, which, allowing for a margin of statistical error, places the two broadly on a par with each other. Across the UK, Spanish comes third, usually some 10%–15% behind German, followed by Italian, which in turn is about 10% behind Spanish.

Most of the UK's export business is currently with EU countries so it is not surprising that the languages most frequently used by UK international companies are French and German, followed by Spanish and Italian. However, it emerges from the LNTO/CILT language skills audits that there are also skill deficiencies in German, Spanish and Italian. Much is made of the over-emphasis in our system on French but the LNTO/CILT language skills audits contain many cases of failure to communicate even with the French often due not only to a lack of good French, or the false expectation that they will speak English. However, prejudice about the French is not uncommon.

The number of companies declaring they use exotic, non-Western European languages (mainly Japanese, Chinese and Russian) is still very small. For example, Japanese is the fifth most widely used language by companies in North West, South West of England and Scotland and in sixth position in North East of England, Northern Ireland, West Midlands, and Wales, following the major Western European languages. Chinese has been of growing importance for a number of years and is rated notably high in Yorkshire and the Humber (fifth), Scotland, Wales and East of England (sixth). Dutch appears to be more widespread in the East of England, relative to other parts of the country, as German does in Scotland, North East England and the West Midlands. In Northern Ireland, Dutch and Korean appear to be in wider use than Italian. Chinese poses problems for more companies in the North West, East, Yorkshire and the Humber, and North East of England. Russian is an additional apparent deficiency in Yorkshire and the Humber, East and North West of England.

Languages in use in Europe

The situation facing many companies based in other parts of Europe is seemingly more straightforward. There is little question that English is the most dominant foreign language in use and English is well established in most continental European schools. But this masks the true picture as many other languages are also in regular use (see Figure 23 in Appendix 1).

So anyone intending to work abroad who expects to get by with English alone will find that languages other than English are commonly used for business in Europe.

For example, the REFLECT findings indicate that German is much used by Polish companies; and French and Spanish by Portuguese companies. With the exception of Spain and Portugal, German appears to be the second lingua franca of European business. It comes second or third to either English or French for most countries in the samples. Scandinavia, the Netherlands and Eastern Europe, in particular, seem to use German significantly. This can be explained by the prominence of Germany as the largest single market in the European Union, but more importantly it also shows that non-English speaking companies outside the UK and Ireland do not necessarily use English when trading with Germany.

The third most used language across the European samples is either French or Spanish, depending on the country, though the existence of Russian as the third language in use in Poland heralds a potential change in the patterns of second language use as the European Union spreads eastwards and more countries join from the former Warsaw Pact where Russian was widespread.

No non-European languages appear in the top-ten languages in use in the samples studied in Sweden, Denmark, Germany, Poland or Portugal, which possibly indicates not only how Euro-centric trade has become for many smaller companies, but may also suggest that continental European companies, too, have been put off by non-European language barriers. The availability of language skills among the workforce appears markedly greater in Poland and Portugal, i.e. 20% higher than in England and 30% higher than in Ireland. By contrast, the UK stands in a potentially strong position with access to a wealth of non-European languages among its ethnically diverse population, and making better use of these vast hidden resources is one of the challenges to which UK businesses and education systems can respond.

International communication, needs and strategies in British business

Internationally trading UK companies (exporters, importers or companies with future trading plans in non-English speaking countries) have been the subject of a series of language surveys over the past decade, due to growing evidence that trade was being lost or missed, as a consequence of language and culture barriers. At the same time the ongoing process of globalisation and the increase in market competitiveness have encouraged companies, both small and large, to trade in foreign markets in all continents leading to more diverse language and cultural demands. The ten new EU accession countries, for example, offer a market opportunity of 75 million consumers and 740,000 sq km of tariff-free territory, but many UK companies will have yet to learn how to handle the new languages and cultures if they are to succeed. This will accelerate further the process of internationalisation as companies have increasingly to 'think global and act local'.

'Acting local' means developing strategies to overcome the linguistic and cultural obstacles posed by foreign and often distant markets. One of the key findings of the studies summarised here is that the means of achieving this for many companies is an **international communication strategy**. This involves developing a strategy that integrates all communication tasks, including new tasks, such as localising products, hiring local staff, or handling foreign enquiries and developing the capability to operate effectively in the local language and culture. However, it is clear that companies can be at different stages of international export development: the reactive, versus proactive, exporter is a well-established concept. The same applies to their awareness of international communication strategies.

All the studies featured in this book add international communications as a significant dimension to our understanding of successful export practice. For example, the LNTO/CILT language skills audits investigate and measure and identify good practice in companies in using international communication strategies, while, by comparison, the objective of the British Chambers of Commerce language survey (2004) was to identify and segment the different behaviours and attitudes held by individual exporters in relation to trading in overseas markets and profile them. The British Chambers of Commerce Language Survey found, for example, that different behaviours on the part of exporters, including use of languages, relate to different types of export performance in their companies. Though the framework still needs further empirical work, it does provide a useful model for describing behaviours, particularly language and culture.

The British Chambers of Commerce Language Survey makes reference to the four types of exporter behaviour:

- **Opportunists**, who just respond to approaches from foreign clients rather than initiate business developments, most often failing to adapt and localise their product to their market and communicating only in English.
- **Developers**, who tend to adapt their products and services more readily to foreign markets but remain reactive towards export development and communicate in English.
- **Adaptors**, who make an effort to adjust their products and services to their foreign markets, have sales literature in the customer's languages and have penetrated a wide range of markets.
- **Enablers**, who are proactive in their exporting, consciously select markets and adapt their products, services and literature to meet the markets. They place a great deal of importance on staff within their business having foreign language skills.

The most important finding of the British Chambers of Commerce language survey for this study is a direct correlation between the value the individual exporter places on language skills in business and their annual turnover. Only 33% of Opportunists had an annual export turnover above £500k. This increased to 54%

for Developers, 67% for Adapters and 77% for Enablers, who placed the most value on language skills within their business. Moreover, export sales by Opportunists (the segment that least values language skills) showed a decline by an average of £50k a year per exporter, while Enablers' (the segment placing the highest value on language skills) exports showed an increase by an average of £290k a year per exporter. Other studies referred to later in this book have also established a clear link between successful international communication strategies and improved trading performance in companies. A recent survey of Welsh employers found results similar to those found by the British Chambers of Commerce. Companies which are 'naturally bilingual', such as those that are Welsh-speaking and are foreign-owned, tend to demonstrate a greater tendency to handle languages effectively to facilitate their international trade.

A more disturbing finding of the *British Chambers of Commerce language survey* (2004) is that 80% of the export managers who responded cannot competently conduct business dealings overseas in even one foreign language. Exporter deficiencies are clearly more wide-ranging than just lack of language skills. Nearly two-thirds of all exporters (63%) apparently have no formal strategy to maintain or instigate trade with foreign speaking businesses and the number with an explicit language or international communication strategy are so few they are almost negligible.

The third key aspect of the British Chambers study is the finding on the importance of early language education: those who learned a second language at primary school are more likely to claim they can conduct business dealings in a foreign language than those who did not. Early language learning is now a feature of Primary School education in most parts of the UK with increasing numbers of bilingual schools in Wales and a well-established Primary School project thriving in Scottish schools. In England entitlement to learning a foreign language from age 7 is a cornerstone of the National Languages Strategy, *Languages for all: Languages for life*.

Furthermore, there has been a need for studies such as those undertaken by the British Chambers of Commerce to investigate the impact of the changes which have taken place in educational provision on trade. The government and informed members of language groups have been concerned about the decline in the already low number of young people studying modern languages beyond the age of 16 and the overall level of general language skills among the UK population. In 2002 the number of pupils taking GCSE French was down by 2.5% and GCSE German by 6.6% by comparison with a downturn in the number of A level language students (down by 13% for French and 17% for German between 2001 and 2002) and a resulting reduction in the number of modern languages graduates, which in turn has threatened the future of teacher training courses in several universities. Schools and Colleges have been suffering too; many educational institutions have struggled to find and employ sufficient modern language teachers.

Positive educational initiatives which support the needs of export companies are the Pathfinder projects, the Languages Ladder and the well-established Specialist Language Colleges scheme, initiatives that are discussed below in 'Changing educational provision'. Other actions will follow in the wake of the Tomlinson Report (2004).

The National Languages Strategy (2002) recognises the link between economic competitiveness and employees who have the necessary language skills, but the means to achieving the development of those skills within present systems is less clearly articulated. UKTI is supporting the continuing development of the successful Export Communications Review scheme (ECR) managed by the British Chambers of Commerce and recently extended to other parts of Europe under the European Union's Leonardo da Vinci programme, PROTOCOL2. The Export Communications Review scheme has delivered over 1,000 export communication reviews to assist UK export companies with their international communication strategies.

Other possible ways ahead for supporting UK internationally trading companies in the medium to long term are apparent from the findings of the studies brought together in this book, and from the recommendation, embedded in the key points at the each of each chapter. It should go without saying that any initiative has to be based on research rather than anecdote and take account of current trends and gaps. In this regard the studies provide an important baseline of the UK's current business language capability from which to move forward.

What is the nature of language barriers facing companies?

The fact that the British Chambers of Commerce found that 80% of the export managers could not competently conduct their business dealings overseas in even one foreign language is a disturbing reflection on UK industry's communication capability. For many, language knowledge is limited to very rudimentary French. The Metra Martech study (1999) also found that the foreign language proficiency of the home-based staff of UK export companies had declined since the previous 1997 survey, confirming a downward trend.

More specific cases and examples of how and why UK companies meet language barriers appear frequently in many of the LNTO/CILT language skills audits (see Chapter 3). Companies tend to need language skills for particular situations: **telephoning** and **meetings** emerge as key occasions, followed by **negotiating**, **correspondence**, **presentations** and **exhibitions**. For example, over two in five internationally trading small-to-medium-sized companies claim to have encountered language barriers, compared with the one in five who knowingly have encountered cultural obstacles in international trade.

These findings are broadly comparable across all parts of Britain: England and Wales (language: 46% and culture: 20%); Scotland (language: 50%; culture: 17% – although the sample is small) and Northern Ireland (language: 38% and culture: 24%). They also concur with the findings of the Metra Martech language study (1999), where 44% of exporters viewed languages as at least a partial barrier to trade. It should further be noted that these figures are likely to be an underestimation due to both the tendency for people to understate their mistakes and inadequacies, as well as to a general lack of awareness of cultural issues.

Do language barriers really occasion lost business?

On average, just over a fifth of companies (21%) in the English and Welsh sample (LNTO/CILT language skills audits) and a small but significant percentage of the Scottish and Northern Irish samples (6% and 14% respectively) acknowledge that they have knowingly lost business as a direct consequence of language or cultural deficiencies. The highest figure is for companies in the East of England (25%), followed by the North West (22%) and the West Midlands (22%). The lowest percentage declaring lost business, apart from Scotland, which had a low response rate, is for the North East of England (19%) and Wales (19%).

Findings vary across other studies. In the Metra Martech study 7% of companies, representing all sizes of exporter (SME to large company) across all regions, indicated they had lost business. However, the authors of the study regard this as almost certainly an understatement of the real business loss. The British Chambers of Commerce language survey (2004) claims a figure of 4% for companies losing business specifically due to language barriers, i.e. not including cultural barriers. The British Chambers of Commerce Survey also found that four out of five exporters claim to have missed or lost sales (or revenue) for various reasons like 'failure to adapt to the market', where communication failure is implied, but not explicitly measured.

In reality, international communication barriers can be at the heart of a wide range of business problems: chasing payments, misunderstanding orders, managing an agent or failing to answer telephone calls, to name but a few. These reasons are not usually identified explicitly as international communication problems when survey findings are collated.

How significant are cultural barriers?

For a number of companies cultural barriers can be at least as significant an obstacle as languages. In earlier studies such as Metra Martech (1997 and 1999) the percentage of international companies in the UK facing cultural barriers is consistently one in five. This is also true for the more recent LNTO/CILT language skills audits, where the figure is 20% for England and Wales. In ELISE (2001) it is 24% for Northern Ireland and 17% for Scotland. Companies facing cultural barriers cite Japan as the trading partner top of the list where obstacles are encountered (16%), followed by France (12%), the Middle East (12%), China (11%) and Germany (9%). France is the highest most frequently mentioned European market giving rise to cultural barriers. Business etiquette, management style, meetings and social behaviour are the most frequently cited generic categories posing problems (see Chapter 4).

As with the figure for language barriers, however, the number of companies facing cultural barriers is probably much higher than the data suggests, because of the flaws of self-reporting. On the other hand, the Metra Martech study (1999) does suggest a higher percentage with 30% of companies of various sizes facing cultural barriers. While this finding is 10% higher than for most other surveys, it serves to highlight cultural issues as a growing challenge for internationally trading companies.

International communication strategies

Success for many companies will depend on formulating an effective international communication strategy. At the moment, only 11% of the English and Welsh employers claim to have an international communication strategy. From the *British Chambers of Commerce language survey* (2004) it is apparent that the two groups of Adaptors and Enablers are the most likely to incorporate the elements of a language strategy within their export strategy. The Enablers, who account for 20% of export managers in the British Chambers of Commerce sample, are the most successful. These are the employers whose companies have shown the greatest export growth in the previous year and who are 'characterised by their proactive export, approach, consciously choosing markets where they want a presence, adapting and localising their products, services and sales literature and placing considerable importance on their UK based staff having foreign language skills' (British Chambers of Commerce, 2004: 10).

Anglocentrics and Opportunists might be encouraged through awareness-raising campaigns like TPUK's National Languages for Export Campaign and schemes like Export Communications Review to become more like the Enabler or Adaptor in their thinking and actions. One obvious obstacle to this happening is the perception of the effectiveness of English-only transactions.

If the East of England is taken as an example, 40% of exporting companies rely on English or the mediation of local English-speaking agents for trading purposes, which seems to imply that 60% use a language other than English. The studies reveal that between 40% and 50% of UK international companies rely heavily on

English for all trading purposes and employ only English-speaking agents, a percentage breakdown that seems to match up to the typology of the British Chambers of Commerce's typology of Anglocentric and Opportunist companies, who unquestioningly rely on English. Companies showing poor exporting performance are more likely to be reliant on English.

A valid strategy for a company trading across many different markets would be to create competence in a small core of intermediary languages which are adaptable to several markets; e.g. French for North Africa; Russian for countries like Belarus and former republics of the USSR; Portuguese for Portugal, parts of southern Africa and Brazil. The development of competence in a core set of world languages would however depend to a large extent on adaptability and capability of the individuals in a given company.

Changing educational provision

The National Languages Strategy argues that England will need competence in the skills to interact in many languages and across many cultures. Knowledge of French will continue to be valuable, but other languages, such as Modern Standard Chinese or Brazilian Portuguese are growing in importance. In a 2004 survey by the recruitment agency Office Angels it was found that Chinese language skills are increasingly needed by employers. Capability in a range of languages is crucially important for the UK to grow economically in an environment driven by international trade and the imperatives of global business operations.

Currently, however, even a modest range of languages such as French, German and Spanish may not have a secure future in many secondary schools. Modern foreign languages were removed from the core curriculum in England for fourteen to sixteen year-olds in September 2004. That means children are now able for the first time in decades to drop languages at the age of fourteen. While the recently published final report of the Tomlinson Working Group on 14–19 Reform recommends that languages be taken into account for all learning programmes 14–16 and continue as an entitlement 16–19, the recommendations will take some time to be implemented in full. The English Government is funding a range of measures to boost uptake of languages among younger age groups at primary schools in England but this, too, will take some years to have any discernible impact among older learners and eventual employees.

In England the DfES's programme is focusing, for example, on primary languages entitlement and secondary initiatives including Pathfinder projects, Specialist Language Colleges and the 'Languages Ladder', which are designed to provide opportunities to motivate learners and promote greater uptake and continuation of language learning at all ages. The 'Language Ladder' recognises language achievement and grades learning rather like the grades traditionally associated with learning a musical instrument. It has six levels, building from 'breakthrough' to 'mastery' and is mapped against the National Qualifications Framework and the Common European Framework. Following the pilot schemes, the Languages Ladder is being extended to cover a further five languages: Italian, Chinese, Japanese, Punjabi and Urdu. In future, a further thirteen languages will be added: Arabic, Bengali, Gaelic/Irish, Gujarati, Hindi, Greek, Polish, Portuguese, Russian, Somali, Swedish, Turkish and Welsh.

In terms of diversification of languages in the secondary sector, more than 200 designated Specialist Language Colleges (SLCs) in England provide a major boost for the future, each offering a range of languages and including some rarer ones (Japanese, Chinese). The Early Language Learning initiative is extending languages to a wide range of primary schools in England, following Scotland's pioneering work in the Primary phase.

At tertiary level, University Language Centres are accounting for a significant increase in the range of languages taught. Numbers of students learning a language alongside their main degree discipline continue steadily to rise. However, there is need for action in mainstream education, where the specialist Languages degree has been in decline for nearly a decade. The decline is contrary to trends elsewhere leading to fewer languages graduates with advanced skills. There is evidence in the work of Kedia and Daniel (2003) of a need for growing internationalisation of education generally. US companies, for example, are now placing greater emphasis on international competence: i.e. 80% of the companies surveyed by the Center for International Business Education and Research at the University of Memphis in 2002 indicated they would place greater emphasis on international competence, which includes linguistic competence, among their staff over the next ten years, emphasising the need for changes in both secondary as well as further and higher education. Languages degrees and degrees with a substantial language component have traditionally offered opportunities for students to enhance their skills by spending time studying or working abroad.

Yet Kedia's and Daniel's work confirms the earlier findings of Webb, Mayer, Pioche and Allen (1999) who argued that all business students require international training and Hoffman and Gopinath (1994) who confirm that CEOs have increasingly recognised how international understanding is a success factor for their firms. Early work by Moxon, O'Shea, Brown and Escher (1997) demonstrates how global awareness and cultural sensitivity are invaluable international skills. Despite the body of international research going back over ten years, there has been a steady decline in the number of overseas placements offered or taken up in UK higher education. In parallel to the rapid decline of take-up for Modern Languages degrees this has resulted in relatively few indigenous young people in Britain entering the job market with either advanced language skills acquired through the education system or international experience.

What does the future look like?

For UK companies

The Government's National Languages Strategy for England, published in December 2002, calls for Regional Development Agencies and Learning and Skills Councils to work with LNTO/CILT and the Regional Language Networks to develop strategies to improve our language capability. The Northwest was the first Regional Development Agency to focus strategically on language skills for business and the majority of other Regional Development Agencies, the Scottish Executive and the Welsh Assembly are now taking up this challenge. The key recommendations included in Chapter 5 provide a basis for further effective action.

On another level, the key to developing communication strategies in companies is more about changing the culture and mindset of personnel, which in turn will lead to a new set of actions. While the LNTO/CILT language skills audits have proposed the actions a company might take in the form of an international communication strategy; for example, translating sales literature, employing native speakers, culturally adapting the website and training, the real challenge is to move the awareness of Opportunists through to that of Developers, then Developers through to Adaptors and Adaptors to Enablers. Growing awareness of the language issue will also lead to more effective export strategies.

For the individual

With increasing globalisation the majority of young people entering the job market today can expect either to work abroad or to come into contact with non-English speaking clients or suppliers, or to be managed here by a foreign company, for some period of their working lives. The companies or organisations where they work are also likely to be in a global alliance, and almost certainly be involved in international collaboration projects, to have a global supply chain. If they do not have linguistic and cultural competence, their future career prospects may be started, or reduced in cases where their company is located abroad, or where it passes into foreign ownership.

The findings of the Kedia and Daniel (2003) study point clearly to an international future for many individuals. Indeed, with the projected growth of international operations for many companies, additional international education programmes will need to be developed, particularly programmes with a focus on new growth markets in Asia and Central and Eastern Europe. At the very least, as citizens of the wider European Union all individuals should have an appreciation for cross-cultural differences and be attuned to a more global perspective.

one

The use of languages by UK business

How widespread is language usage in UK companies?

At first glance the number of companies with language skills in this country appears higher than expected. For example, from various studies (e.g. LNTO/CILT language skills audits, ELISE) it seems that well over half of the international companies surveyed in the UK and trading in non-English speaking markets claim to use at least one foreign language (see Figure 3 overleaf). In some regions the figure is even higher; the West Midlands records the highest percentage (70%), while Yorkshire and the Humber, Scotland, Northern Ireland and Wales are all in the 52%–54% bracket. The average for England and Wales is 60% and therefore appears strong. The issue here is for companies to recognise what constitutes effective competence in a language.

Despite the initially encouraging signs of a high volume of UK companies using a foreign language in international trade, this gives a misleading picture. The Metra Martech study (1999) found that the foreign language proficiency of the home-based staff of UK export companies had actually declined since 1997. From the many case studies in the LNTO/CILT language skills audits it is also clear that only a few companies have consciously integrated languages into their export strategy (these would be the British Chamber of Commerce's Enablers) and that levels of proficiency are far from high, with many companies 'muddling through', often with only rudimentary French.

On the surface, the 40% or so of companies not using any foreign languages would seem to be coping without the need for foreign language capability. Indeed, many companies use English for all their traditional trading purposes, such as the British Chamber of Commerce's Anglocentric companies, and appear not to suffer unduly. However, what matters to the UK in the medium-term is whether this apparent deficiency is ultimately damaging to the companies concerned and to the UK's economic competitiveness. The answer surely lies in the underlying trends. Are more companies having to resort to using the customer's language and how, if at all, has the picture changed in response to changing world markets over the last five years?

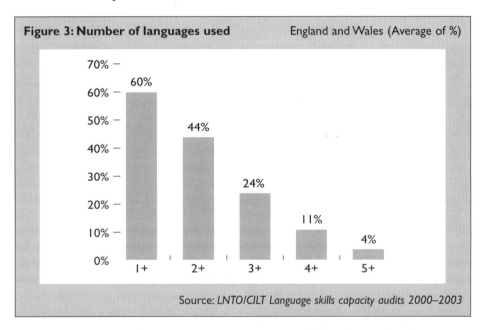

Figure 3: Number of languages used — England and Wales (Average of %)

Source: *LNTO/CILT Language skills capacity audits 2000–2003*

The trend apparent in the LNTO/CILT language skills audits is towards the multiple use of languages by an increasing minority of companies at the 'more proficient end'. Over four in ten companies (i.e. 44% in England and Wales) now regularly use two or more foreign languages for trade and approximately a quarter of the sample claim to be using at least three or more foreign languages; and about one in 25 use five or more. As companies have to trade more widely to capture markets in an increasingly competitive global environment, so the trend will have to continue towards companies acquiring a multilingual capability if they are to survive.

Other studies, such as a recent report by ACCAC (1999), have also established a clear link between bilingualism in companies and improved trading performance.

Companies which are 'naturally bilingual like Welsh companies have also demonstrated a greater tendency to deploy foreign languages to facilitate international trade as in the case of findings from a sub-sample of 37 Welsh inward investor companies in the LNTO/CILT Welsh language skills audit.

This is further borne out, at least in terms of language use, in other LNTO/CILT language skills audits; e.g. the South West of England (69 companies) and the East of England (62), which suggest that foreign-owned companies based in the UK are more aware of the need to use languages than are home-grown businesses. One of the reasons for this is that foreign-owned companies are frequently already international in outlook and their trade strategy usually follows a multilingual approach in policy and practice. For example, SuperH, the UK subsidiary of a Californian-owned company, very clearly recognises that there is much value to be gained by having in-house language proficiency, at least 'as a tool to expand business'.

case study

SUPERH (UK) Ltd, South West England

Company: a subsidiary of a California company, employing 60 staff and exporting 80% of its product worldwide. The parent company, the UK subsidiary and the Japanese subsidiary are operationally equal.

Product: micro-electronic designs and components.

Example of customer base: Hitachi and ST Micro-Electronics (a Franco-Italian company).

Although it is true that the overall level of English is high in this sector of activity and the company's written contract work and technical literature tends to be in English, they nevertheless attach great importance to languages. They have good French, Italian and Japanese skills in-house and state that languages are 'a tool to expand our business'. They recognise that if they can deploy fluent French they can more easily gain access to a possible French customer.

They have not, to date, experienced linguistic or cultural barriers because they focus on markets for which they have a good knowledge of the language or native speakers working for them. They do, however, try to raise cultural awareness. This figured in a recent California meeting of representatives of the three sister companies. An example of their appreciation of cultural difference was that an approach to a new Japanese company would be made at a very high level in the first instance, as opposed to an initial meeting of technical staff, as might happen with a North American or European company.

They intend to expand into other South East Asian markets like Taiwan and would set out to retain someone with good local language skills, as well as technical expertise, for preference a Taiwanese rather than a locally domiciled European.

They recruit their staff from across Europe and candidates with language skills are favourably viewed. About 20% of their staff have languages and training is also offered. Currently an external trainer comes to the company to give one hour per week of Japanese to anyone who wants it. (This is to give staff the basics 'so that they know where the station is when they travel).'

They have not normally been required to translate any literature, except on one occasion when a Japanese customer asked for a Japanese version of technical data to pass on to a customer.

Source: LNTO/CILT South West of England language skills capacity audit

Which languages are most frequently used?

Not surprisingly, the large majority of languages referred to in the qualitative case studies are European, where 'mainly French, German and Italian' are cited (Wales); while the four dominant languages are also referred to as 'the usual suspects' in an interview with a translation company in the East of England. The Metra Martech study (1999) also confirms these four are in most general use, though the percentage of companies using French and German is lower than in the LNTO/CILT language skills audits.

French and German have consistently remained the two most widely used languages mentioned across all surveys of the UK. French comes out as the most widely used foreign language, followed closely by German, (e.g. see Figure 4 opposite for England and Wales: French 45%; German 36%). There are a few regional variations: in Scotland and the North East of England, for example, the margin of difference between companies using French and German is only 1% which, allowing for statistical error, places the two broadly on a par with each other. Spanish comes third in use, usually some 10–15% behind German, followed by Italian at some 10% behind Spanish. Northern Ireland is the exception; use of Dutch and Korean appear greater than use of Italian.

Paradoxically French, while cited as the most used foreign language by companies, also poses significant language and cultural barriers. Moreover, somewhat surprisingly, Dutch appears fifth in overall usage, which suggests that even traditionally 'English-speaking' parts of the world cannot necessarily be treated as English native speaking areas. In these cases, however, it is often specialist register that is required, e.g. instructions for dealing with Dutch lorry drivers or words for handling particular cargoes. On a social level, words for general conversation (breaking the ice) can be a bonus. Just a few words of a less widely spoken language like Dutch can elicit a positive reaction from Dutch clients.

There are significant variations in the parts of the UK where individual languages are used and much has to do with trading patterns. For example, Dutch appears

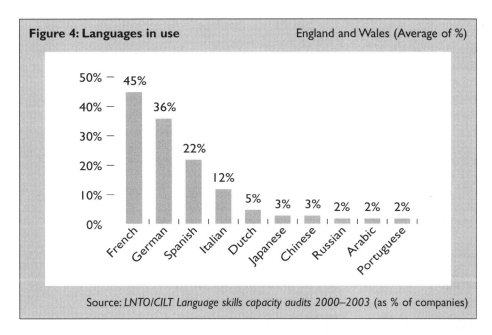

Figure 4: Languages in use   England and Wales (Average of %)

Source: *LNTO/CILT Language skills capacity audits 2000–2003* (as % of companies)

to be more widely used in the East of England; and German is used by relatively more companies from Scotland, North East and the West Midlands. Traditional trading links between the Netherlands and East Anglia, and manufacturing engineering links between the industrialised North East, Scotland, West Midlands and Germany may explain this. While there is a need for further research to investigate whether or not these traditional trading patterns will hold in future, if they will, then this may suggest that there is an argument for schools and universities to adapt provision in the languages curriculum to the language needs of their local area, or region. For example, the East of England (notably, East Anglia) might offer greater provision in German and Dutch, due to its traditional links with these parts of the world.

However, the range of foreign languages in overall trading use across the country is not very large, given the multilingual nature of the growing global market. The issue that many smaller companies face is one of how to formulate an international communication strategy from within limited resources. How does a small company, for example, acquire the language skills to trade effectively in, say, ten target markets? However, the company may not have to acquire ten different languages since there is no one-to-one correlation between the trade destination and use of the local language. This apparent paradox is clearly illustrated by the use of English as a lingua franca. For example, some countries are very open to the use of English, even when they are buying (as opposed to selling) goods, notably in Scandinavia, the Netherlands and parts of Germany. So a company faced with a bewilderingly large number of languages in the global market can still consider developing a holistic strategy which may require acquiring high-level capability in the languages of its two or three main markets, together with studious use of international English and other intermediary languages. In its portfolio, however, there would invariably need to be one or two non-European languages.

Use of non-European languages

At a cursory glance, current demand for non-European languaes does not appear great. However, this is also driven by the virtual negligible capability of British companies in these rarer languages.

The number of companies declaring they use non-European languages, mainly Japanese, Chinese and Russian, is very small. For example, Japanese is the language fifth most widely used by companies in the North West of England, South West of England and Scotland and is in sixth position in the North East of England, Northern Ireland, West Midlands, and Wales, following the major European languages. Chinese is of growing importance, notably in Yorkshire and the Humber (fifth) and in Scotland, Wales and East of England (sixth). This is also a reflection of changing UK trading patterns (see Figure 6) and suggests there is a need to develop a greater capability in these languages than is currently the case. For example the size and potential of the Chinese market appears not to have hit British companies yet. In these markets British companies currently have little choice other than to communicate in English, often via UK-based native speakers or market-based intermediaries. However, companies seeking to penetrate markets in East Asia will almost inevitably have to develop much greater linguistic and cultural competence if they intend to trade there in the longer term, as the growth potential of these markets cannot be ignored.

In which situations do companies use their languages?

Broadly, there are nine business situations (see Figure 5 opposite) where companies tend to need language skills. *Telephoning* and *meetings* emerge as key occasions when companies need language skills to make and maintain contact with clients. *Negotiating* and *correspondence*, *presentations* and *exhibitions* may sometimes involve 'harder' skills and require translators or interpreters. Indeed, a professional linguist, or local agent, is absolutely necessary for certain critical situations where contracts are under discussion, especially in the negotiation and finalising of deals.

People at the interface – involved in face-to-face meetings or direct telephone contact – are certainly more likely to need more spontaneous, unplanned foreign language capability than those, for example, engaged in fax or e-mail communication. Unfortunately, few UK companies have these skills on hand,

Figure 5

Rank order of usage	Situation
1	Telephoning
2	Meetings
3	Negotiating
4	Correspondence
5	Travelling
6	Exhibitions
7	Socialising
8	Presentations
9	Technical literature

such as at the reception or on the switchboard, and can rarely respond **spontaneously** in a foreign language. The interface flashpoint is one of the commonest causes of barriers.

Handling **technical literature**, such as specifications, appears only in ninth place among the most frequent situations because companies almost always have to (and should) engage specialists for this purpose, which is normally beyond the scope of most company employees, even native speakers. However, the cost of relying on language professionals can often be prohibitive for a small firm starting out in a new foreign market. Introducing an outsider or language professional as an intermediary can also put a strain on the development of a direct relationship between client and supplier. Finding the right person for this kind of job is one area of support where some companies have found the UKTI's 'Passport to Export' scheme invaluable.

The case studies in the LNTO/CILT surveys also illustrate how companies cope with international communication blockages. Sometimes a little language can go a long way; the need to know some basic expressions such as words of greeting or travel terms is referred to by several case study interviewees, including in a company in the East of England, who state that 'being nice or polite in the customer's own language' and 'enough of the language to get past the switchboard and in contact with a fluent English speaker is extremely useful'. When travelling, even a few words in the local language, like 'right' or 'left' can dramatically reduce stress levels and uncertainty. Too little language can, however, also raise false expectations.

A company in the South West has one person with some language ability who may be said to be doing a little better than 'muddling through': 'I still have problems with languages', [however] we mostly get by and customers seem to appreciate the effort'.

Languages and trade destinations

Limited though it can be, capability in European languages is vital to improving the UK's current trading balance. In the Welsh language skills capacity audit, for example, fourteen out of the 21 key foreign non-English speaking export markets cited are in Europe, which may be said to be typical across the UK, since the EU accounts for more than 60% of the UK's export sales. The need for companies to become more Europeanised and the need for skills in a range of European languages is becoming more and more apparent. Greater mobility in Europe is greatly assisting UK companies with the process of acquiring a market-oriented outlook, but perhaps more importantly there is an increasing number of native speakers taking jobs in British companies who not only help to handle language issues but, in the process, act as change agents for their company's internationalisation.

In terms of trade turnover, Germany (see Figure 6) remains the current most important non-English speaking market for 46% of small businesses in England and Wales, followed by France (45%); in Scotland France is favoured by 34% and Germany by 31%, while in Northern Ireland, France and Germany are first-equal at 34% (see Figure 6). Across the English regions alone France and Germany are also the most important non-English speaking trading areas, followed by the Netherlands (31%), Spain (27%), Italy (26%), the Middle East (23%), South East Asia (21%), Sweden (20%), Central and Eastern Europe (20%) and Japan (13%).

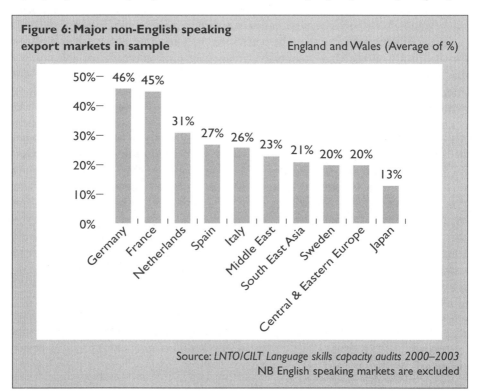

Figure 6: Major non-English speaking export markets in sample   England and Wales (Average of %)

Source: LNTO/CILT Language skills capacity audits 2000–2003
NB English speaking markets are excluded

The Netherlands, Scandinavia and parts of Germany are often referred to as 'soft', or starter, markets because the language barrier is less pronounced. This is mainly because there is often little stigma attached to using English for selling, as well as buying, largely because of the close cultural affinity between these countries and the UK. Two Welsh companies commented on how certain countries are happy to trade with them in English: 'Swedes are happy to deal in English. The Dutch (want) to show off their perfect English'; and 'The Germans by and large speak English' .

As a guiding principle, however, selling into a non-native, but traditionally English-speaking market is always easier if the UK company has those foreign language skills on site: 'Even Swedish customers with their good English like to speak Swedish if they will be understood' (North West of England). Companies which are more advanced in their international communication strategies tend to create competence in a core of so-called **intermediary languages** which are adaptable to several markets; e.g. French in North Africa; Russian in Belarus and certain republics of the former Soviet Union, such as Kazakhstan or Uzbekistan.

An intermediary language can be beneficial provided cultural sensitivities permit. While it appears a logical second language to use, Russian, for example, may not necessarily be a good choice in countries which are celebrating their release from Soviet hegemony, e.g. countries like Poland, Latvia and Lithuania. German can be a useful lingua franca in Central Europe. For one East of England company, 'Afrikaans also works in various places', including Africa, the Netherlands and Flemish speaking Europe.

An export challenge facing many UK companies is expansion into eight Central and Eastern European Union accession countries where English has not traditionally been spoken even as a commercial lingua franca. In these new environments, UK companies have to perform a variety of tasks in the local language; e.g. open outlets, go into joint ventures, or acquire companies in the east. The imperative for companies and organisations to become multilingual is becoming acute; managers who are seconded abroad to other parts of Europe are managing workforces which are themselves polyglot and they have to learn to deal not just with local cultural issues, but with cross-cultural working environments, as trading patterns extend to embrace more areas of the world.

One company that has had major success in Eastern Europe is Whittle Eastern Europe Logistics Ltd.

Whittle Eastern Europe Logistics Ltd (Clitheroe), North West England

This is a small Freight Forwarder business with fifteen staff and a turnover of £13 million. They deal between hauliers, airlines and shipping companies on the one hand and manufacturers on the other. Goods are forwarded into, as well as out of, the UK. The main export market is, by far, Central and Eastern Europe. They work for big companies like ICI and British Steel, and also for other freight forwarders.

The Managing Director, accounts and marketing staff are British but the operations staff are all foreign: Czech, Slovak, Hungarian, Belorussian, Ukrainian, Polish, Latvian, Croatian.

They do encounter language barriers but they can overcome them with their in-house linguistic ability. The staff are mostly multilingual, with at least three languages including good English. It is also the case, as the Managing Director puts it, that his staff 'are mad keen on languages anyway' and often wish to add other languages. They employ many foreign spouses of British workers.

The company can also encounter cultural barriers but the staff are in a position to understand the different cultures. Business extends as far as Uzbekistan and Kazakhstan. German is useful because they find Czechs, Slovaks and several others often speak German: 'They may perhaps be anti-German but for business purposes they will use the language'.

If the company were to expand into new markets, the policy would remain one of recruiting the appropriate native speakers. With this staffing policy the company has to search widely in the UK to get replacements.

Source: LNTO/CILT North West of England language skills capacity audit

What changes are future trading patterns likely to bring?

Over two in five (43%) of the English and Welsh survey respondents declared they intended to trade in new non-English speaking markets, which was similar to the proportion of Scottish (46%) and Northern Irish (44%) companies. Figure 7 opposite lists the key future non-English speaking target markets for the regions and national administrations of the UK. Central and Eastern Europe, Latin America, Europe and China feature strongly, while Germany and France will remain important as has traditionally been the case.

Even though non-European markets are known to pose potentially greater language and cultural challenges, they are undoubtedly the growth markets of the future. This particularly applies to markets such as Latin America, Eastern and Central Europe, as well as China and South East Asia. It is the high growth markets in these regions where new exporters can expect to meet most international communication barriers, yet have least language and cultural capability. Currently they have to rely most heavily on intermediaries for their language needs. In other words, the future is likely to be more rather than less demanding in international communication terms.

Figure 7: Future intended trading regions

Region/Country	No. of UK regions or national administrations in LNTO Studies placing this region as first target
Central and Eastern Europe	3
Latin America	3
Europe	2
China	2
France	1
Region/Country	**No. of UK regions or national administrations placing this region as second target**
China	3
Germany	3
Latin America	3
France	1
Others: Spain, Middle East, Central Europe	1

Source: *LNTO/CILT Language skills capacity audits 2000–2003*
NB Some UK areas indicated more than one preferred country/continent

Which foreign languages are used in other European countries?

The surveys have found evidence that several languages other than English are widely used for trade across Europe. In particular, German is much used by Polish companies; French and Spanish by Portuguese companies. Poland and Portugal use a few languages with greater frequency than either England or Ireland. No non-European languages appear in the Swedish, Danish, German, Polish and Portuguese 'top ten' of most-used languages, which indicates not only how Euro-centric trade may be for this sample of companies, but may also suggests the strong possibility that many continental European companies have, like their counterparts, yet to address non-European language barriers.

The availability of language skills among the workforce appears markedly greater in Poland and Portugal, 20% higher than in England and 30% higher than in Ireland. Other than in Spain, Portugal and, of course, Germany, German is very strongly positioned as a major intermediary language of European business. It comes second or third to either English or French for most countries in the sample. Scandinavia, the Netherlands and Eastern Europe, in particular, seem to use German significantly. This can be explained by the prominence of Germany as the largest single market in the European Union, but it also shows that non-English speaking companies outside the UK and Ireland do not necessarily use English when trading with Germany. The third most used language across the companies is either French or Spanish, though the appearance of Russian as the third language in use in Poland by Polish companies demonstrates how the multilingual trading map of Europe is expanding eastwards.

Do UK companies have the on-site language capability to trade globally?

Of the employees with language skills in the UK companies surveyed, 39% have French, 26% German and 13% Spanish. Fewer than 7% have any Italian and a tiny number have competence in another rarer language, i.e. Dutch, Arabic, Portuguese or Russian. Knowledge of German is highest in the manufacturing areas of Northern England and the Midlands. The four traditionally most frequently learned Western European languages (French, German, Spanish, Italian) are invariably the ones most referred to in the case studies. The situation broadly reflects education provision; but it seems the case that German, Spanish and Italian are less available than would be desirable for trading purposes. The statement from a key stakeholder in the East of England suggests that the overall figure for language competence is even less impressive 'if you strip out French done by most people at school'.

There is evidence of a worrying decline in skills in many languages. From the subset of the 503 respondents who possess language skills and who took part in the Department of Trade and Industry's (1999) Metra Martech longitudinal studies over a five-year period, there has been a noticeable decline over time in the percentage of companies with proficiency in German and French, and a slight but by no means balancing increase in those with Spanish and Italian (Figure 8 opposite). At a time of increasing multilingualism in global trade the picture in the UK is one of linguistic retrenchment rather than expansion.

Figure 8: European languages in which home based staff are proficient					
% Replying	1994	1995	1996	1997	1999
French	44	46	45	42	34
German	38	38	38	36	29
Spanish	16	13	16	17	18
Italian	9	9	8	9	11

Source: *Metra Martech Language Study* (1999)

Who speaks languages in UK companies?

The main finding in UK export companies is the widespread lack of language skills found at all more junior grades of staff, regardless of the field of operations. Even export staff, as well as customer services staff and sales staff, have negligible language skills.

In Figure 9 overleaf it is the general manager, or Managing Director, rather than the sales manager or export manager, who has some language skills. Nearly two in five of all mentions of skills are among company personnel at this top functional level. There is a major risk to a company's sustainability if the only 'linguist' in the company is the Managing Director. From the research it is frequently the MD who contacts foreign customers, goes to high level meetings and does the most travelling abroad, though one allows for the fact that many trading partners prefer to deal directly with the most senior person before they will sign contracts. However, the MD is not available to handle every foreign caller. The Managing Director of a Welsh company 'does most of the language work himself'; and the two senior managers of another Welsh company are proficient linguists. More sales directors need encouragement to acquire language skills, but so often languages are a low priority in SMEs which are so busy, as a North West of England International Trade Manager put it, 'chasing their tails'. In many European countries it is the secretarial/administrative function that comes out as the leading language resource in companies. In England and Wales this is relatively poor, though falls into second place. Technical and engineering personnel come close behind MD/ Export Managers.

With increases in cross-border joint ventures, take-overs and mergers, both the engineering and technical functions are now much more prominent in their need for languages than has previously been the case. This goes hand in hand with the increasing level of technical support required in global activities, where a British company may need language skills for the follow-up maintenance support for an overseas client or local workforce development.

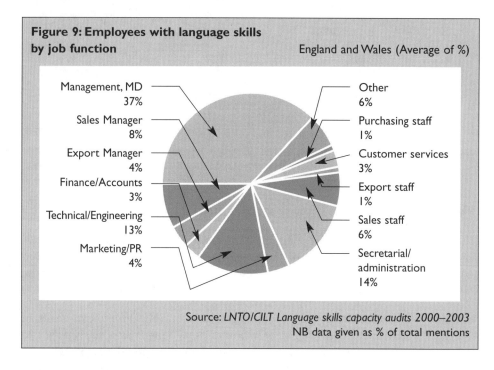

Figure 9: Employees with language skills by job function

England and Wales (Average of %)

Management, MD 37%
Sales Manager 8%
Export Manager 4%
Finance/Accounts 3%
Technical/Engineering 13%
Marketing/PR 4%

Other 6%
Purchasing staff 1%
Customer services 3%
Export staff 1%
Sales staff 6%
Secretarial/administration 14%

Source: *LNTO/CILT Language skills capacity audits 2000–2003*
NB data given as % of total mentions

What is the level of language knowledge among employees?

Few UK companies appear to have the range and depth of language and cultural knowledge required for effective international communication at various levels in the company (see Figure 10). Many employees with language skills declare they are either at basic or intermediate level, where 'intermediate' has, in practice, an undifferentiated approximation to GCSE. Statistically over 50% of the available skills in companies are confirmed to be either at beginner or intermediate level. This means that a large proportion of foreign language speakers in companies can often do little more than 'show willing and be courteous', according to an East of England International Trade Adviser.

The bilingual group and those declaring themselves 'fluent' make up nearly one third of those company respondents with language skills. Case study interviews reveal that the fluent and bilingual groups normally consist of either employees who have lived abroad or non-native speakers of English who have moved to the UK. For example, the Sales and Marketing Director of one East of England company spent five years working in France and speaks directly in French to French customers.

The increase in the number and availability of native speakers of other languages in UK-based companies has had a significant positive impact on companies' language capacity. Some such individuals have gained employment in the UK as a result of

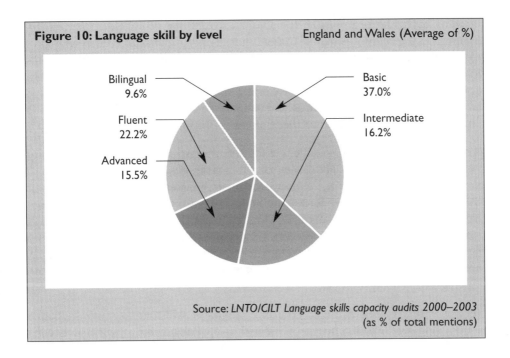

Figure 10: Language skill by level   England and Wales (Average of %)

Bilingual
9.6%

Fluent
22.2%

Advanced
15.5%

Basic
37.0%

Intermediate
16.2%

Source: *LNTO/CILT Language skills capacity audits 2000–2003*
(as % of total mentions)

cross-border mergers and joint ventures, as well as from company secondments of staff from overseas offices to the UK. There are also some special cases, such as the North West exporting company where all the operations staff are native speakers of languages other than English. A second example is the Michelin Shared Service Centre, also in the North West, where the overseas employer requires very high levels of language proficiency and is able to secure these locally, partly by employing large numbers of native speakers. There is no doubt that in the short term further measures are required to encourage more native speakers to work for UK companies as a response to the lack of home-grown language capability. Whether the language deficit of UK companies should lead to a more relaxed approach to immigration is now a matter of debate.

Data on relative competence offers a comparison between England/Wales and six other European countries (see Figure 25 in Appendix 1). The table shows that, though the Irish data may be slightly skewed by the possible inclusion of the Irish language, the England and Wales sample has a broadly similar proportion of employees to Portugal, France, Germany and Spain (about 50%) whose declared language skills are either at basic or intermediate level. The low number of 'advanced speakers' in the English speaking areas compared with the number for other countries simply confirms the trend towards lower levels of attainment in foreign languages at the exit points from our education system.

At the higher levels, it is Managers or Managing Directors in England (and Poland) who speak other languages, and tend to have studied a language to a higher level.

Drawing on evidence from the REFLECT and ELISE data from Portugal, Ireland, France and Germany, it is mainly the secretarial and administrative staff who have a second language. This might suggest that in England (and Poland, which seems to follow England's example!) linguistic skills tend to be a reflection in other European countries of formal tertiary education provision and possibly limited to an elite, whereas in other countries languages have traditionally been available to all, and in the primary and secondary phases of formal schooling.

Low proficiency levels in the UK is a matter of concern. At present, firms have only a very hazy approximate view of what tasks employees can perform in a foreign language. Frequently, employees report language qualifications on their CVs which are meaningless for an employer, particularly if the syllabus does not cover any of the critical tasks required in business. Use of the National Language Standards (a competence framework based on the Council of Europe Common European Framework for the Teaching and Assessing of Modern Languages) is one answer to this issue of benchmarking. Not enough companies have adopted this highly useful system yet.

Various interviewees in the LNTO/CILT language skills audits tend to blame school language learning provision for low proficiency levels at work: 'Everyone should learn more languages at school, but it's hard to get that across' (North West of England).

The Head of Inward Investment of the North West of England Development Agency (North West of England language skills capacity audit) also argued strongly for more languages in schools, with the proviso that 'languages in school should be made ... more enjoyable'. She also argued for more languages via university-wide language schemes and languages as a component of MBA courses. Many of the interviewees in the LNTO case studies do, however, demonstrate they are not up to date, either with recent initiatives in school provision, the success of languages provision in UK university language centres, early learning initiatives in the primary phase or the development of Specialist Language Colleges.

Key points

UK companies clearly lag behind many countries of Europe both in terms of the breadth and depth of their linguistic competence. This deficit facing many companies could seriously impede UK business expansion overseas, particularly in taking advantage of new markets in central and Eastern Europe and East Asia. Some of the more aware companies, containing the Enablers and Adaptors, tend to make up any deficit in their on-site language competence through adopting effective international communication strategies involving a series of measures to address in-company shortfalls in language and cultural skills. This is only one stop-gap solution. Others rely on changes to educational provision.

One positive sign on the horizon is the newly introduced entitlement to language provision in primary schools in England. A key finding from the British Chambers of Commerce language survey (2004) is that those who learnt languages at primary school are more likely to claim they can conduct business in a foreign language. Improvements in learning opportunities at primary school level may ultimately help build language capacity in England. However, this remains a long-term solution.

The immediate challenges facing the UK are:

- how to embed greater language capability among a wider range of employees in the company, especially to meet the need for spontaneous foreign language use;
- how to meet increasing opportunities in the new markets of China and Eastern Europe for which available language and cultural skills in companies are currently negligible.

For the time being, companies would be advised to establish their own international communication strategy as a means of supporting their export strategy.

two

Barriers to trade

Language barriers

Barriers to international communication are often hidden and can go unnoticed by exporters in the wider context of lost export opportunities and lost sales. In the *British Chambers of Commerce language survey* (2004) over three quarters of UK exporters (77%) claim to have missed or lost export sales or revenue over the previous two years, for a wide range of reasons, including language and cultural issues. These include failure to adapt to the market; sending the wrong goods abroad or having them returned; or simply not receiving payment; and, in addition to this, separately identified specific language problems are mentioned.

While the number of companies specifically citing language as a barrier is small in the British Chambers research, each of the other reasons given may also contain a language or cultural component; for example, chasing payment requires use of a foreign language, as does direct marketing. In the LNTO/CILT language skills capacity audits the findings are more precisely defined. Over two in five companies, on average, claim to have encountered language barriers in their international trade and about one in five have encountered cultural obstacles. These findings are broadly comparable across all parts of Britain: England and Wales (language: 46% and culture: 20%); Scotland (language: 50%; culture: 17% –

36

although the sample is small) and Northern Ireland (language: 38% and culture: 24%). These findings mirror those of the Metra Martech (1999), where 44% of 503 exporters viewed languages as at least a partial barrier to trade.

Which languages cause the barriers?

It is not surprising, given the greater frequency of contact, that language barriers are mainly experienced in French, German, Spanish and Italian, a similar pattern found also in the earlier ELUCIDATE study (Hagen, 1999). The LNTO/CILT language skills audits findings in England and Wales can be contrasted with the findings of the ELUCIDATE study (1999: 47). Figure 11 below shows the top ten languages for companies experiencing barriers in the English and Welsh survey population, compared with the findings of the earlier ELUCIDATE study (1999: 47), carried out in three English regions.

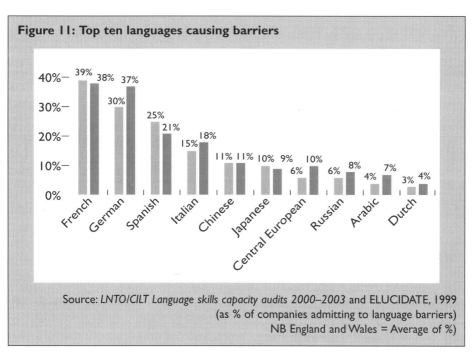

Figure 11: Top ten languages causing barriers

Source: *LNTO/CILT Language skills capacity audits 2000–2003* and ELUCIDATE, 1999
(as % of companies admitting to language barriers)
NB England and Wales = Average of %)

Since 1999 there have been several notable changes:

• German seems, on the surface, to pose less of a barrier in England and Wales than was apparent at the time of the ELUCIDATE study. The English regional samples demonstrate broadly the same pattern of barriers with the exception of the North West and East of England.

- Compared with the ELUCIDATE findings, Spanish seems to have become a barrier for many more companies, while Italian has fallen back a little. In the North West and East of England Spanish now poses a barrier to more companies than German (by a margin of 1%–3%).
- There are clearer regional variations in the LNTO/CILT language skills audits: for example, strong evidence of Polish as a barrier appears in the North East of England and Yorkshire and the Humber (for about one in 20/25 companies); elsewhere it is less of an obstacle.
- Around 10%–11% of companies experience language barriers with either Japanese or Chinese. Barriers with Japanese are now more prevalent. However, Chinese poses problems for more companies in particular regions: the North West (14.7%), East (13.1%), Yorkshire and the Humber (12.7%) and North East of England (12.2%).
- The other less widely known languages causing barriers are: Russian, Arabic and Portuguese. Russian is an apparent deficiency for more companies in Yorkshire and the Humber (7.5%), East (7.2%), North West of England (7.1%).

So, comparing these studies with ELUCIDATE five years on, are the changes meaningful? Allowing for the fact that the data is not parallel and the LNTO/CILT language skills audits offer significantly more data than ELUCIDATE, it is still possible to point to general tendencies. There is a broad consistency in the rank order; French and German are always to the fore. German poses a riddle; apart from the difference in size of datasets, there are two possible explanations for an apparent decline in the number of companies experiencing difficulties with barriers in German: (1) the recent poor performance of the German economy has led to more sluggish Anglo-German trade; and (2) there is an ever increasing willingness to use English in Europe generally, and Germans are generally not averse to speaking English.

What are the causes of barriers?

The causes of the barriers are often down to each company's, and often just one individual's, perceptions. Causes can, therefore, vary from seemingly insignificant misunderstandings to cases of total communication breakdown. In one East of England company, some French visitors understood 'offer' to mean 'free offer'. In another, total communication breakdown came about when Brazilian customers apparently reacted badly to being addressed in Spanish. In the South West of England language skills capacity audit one respondent makes the simple point: 'We usually try to communicate in English, but I believe a certain amount is lost in translation'.

Companies' perceptions of the cause of the barrier range from the general to the specific. The general view that there are '[no problems] as yet, as most people can speak English' (South West of England), may suggest either an Anglocentric or Opportunist approach to international trade. This compares with high levels of awareness in more experienced companies, as exemplified by the businessman in the North East of England: '[we have problems with] German, Swedish, French and Dutch – [and with] phone, meetings and documentation'; or, 'With greater than 90% exports to foreign countries in-house language skills are essential, but a lack in telephone, meeting, presentation and negotiation skills is top of the list [for causing us problems].' (South West of England).

For some companies language barriers seem to be everywhere; '[there are problems with] all languages' (Yorkshire and the Humber). 'We distribute throughout Europe, so unless we can communicate in French, German, Italian, Spanish, Russian, we have encountered barriers.'(East of England) 'We travel to many different destinations therefore we are always going to have some difficulties with communication.' (North East of England).

In other cases, the issue is vaguely acknowledged but otherwise little is known about the specifics of how international communication barriers can affect a company in their bottom line, as with this Scottish company: '[we] cannot quantify or qualify [the language barriers] but it does happen.' It is of course impossible to expect companies to be able to identify and measure the cost of their language deficit on their international trade if they have only ever used English.

Meetings are also high on the list as causes of barriers. Lack of local language knowledge can hinder a meeting or negotiations in a number of ways. Several companies refer to missing the nuances or the little asides that tell the real story. As one company recorded, 'There is a general lack of full detail when talking to foreigners.' (Yorkshire and the Humber). There can also be a sense that some element is missing from dialogues where no one speaks the local language:

- 'In such situations [like meetings] it is impossible to pick up on the throw-away comments that we all make, so important when meeting for the first time. No way of getting a gut feeling.' (East of England)
- 'The majority of customer contacts speak English, but this leads to separate discussions in meetings and a disadvantage in not knowing what the customer is saying/discussing.' (North East of England)

This can also apply when there is an interpreter present who follows the more formal dialogue and misses out the nuances and asides. Non-verbal communication is not generally interpreted. Spontaneous contact causes the most concerns. As already noted, international communication needs at reception or on the switchboard can pose major difficulties, as can impromptu meetings or customer visits; or indeed any situation where there is a need for an on-the-spot response.

There are exceptions, companies who take their international communications seriously, or 'Enablers' such as the modest respondent in a firm in the East of England: 'Only myself in the company (has some skills), I only speak German fluently, semi-fluent French and tourist Spanish'.

Other companies take a minimalist perspective, a few words are acquired as a survival strategy. This company might be said to have adopted at least at one level the strategy of an intermediary language (French) for their market: '[You must] learn a bit of their language. Use bad French in Italy. At least one other language to get you out of trouble'. (West Midlands).

Generally, however, the lack of language skills simply puts potential customers off: 'We find that customers are reluctant to ring us in case they have to explain to someone who doesn't speak their language.' (South West of England).

How valuable is English?

In cases like these, the business person has little idea whether using the local language, instead of just using English, would have created an opportunity or helped them save a lost sale. Occasionally, companies do recognise that an all-English speaking staff at a foreign exhibition can be off-putting, particularly to certain nationalities: 'The fact that we are an English speaking company could have deterred people from visiting our stand at exhibitions, e.g. the Japanese, French' (North East of England). 'We work all over the world and it would be impractical for us to speak or try to speak all languages. Those that might be useful to have a basic command of are: German, Russian and Belgian (=Dutch/Flemish) and possibly French/Spanish'. (North East of England).

However, the barrier may arise in specific trading regions of the world where UK companies cannot easily use English: '[we have problems] with Russian. [There are] few Russian speaking staff and poor English is experienced in Russia'. (North East of England). 'We've only dealt with people who can speak English'. (North East of England). 'I am fed up at sitting in a corner listening to them speaking German and not understanding a word of it'. (South West).

'English-only' approaches remain a two-edged sword; some feel the tactic is invaluable, others see a danger in relying totally on English and question the common assumption that everyone speaks English. A global marketplace suggests a need for skills in a multiplicity of languages, which poses a quandary for most UK companies, which often have neither the time nor the resource (nor the awareness in some cases) to acquire language skills. However, for many, using English is all that they can do at the moment, even though they know that foreign language knowledge is very desirable. The danger for **English-only** companies is the assumption that this language is all they will ever need.

Use of English, as the exclusive language for all trading purposes, is not as widespread as one might expect. If we take the East of England as an example, 40% of exporting companies rely only on English or the intermediation of local English-speaking agents for trading purposes. Certain sectors have adopted English as their lingua franca, which is an undoubted aid to international trade. Respondents frequently make comments such as 'English really is an international language for the medical and veterinarian professions', or 'English is the international technical language', but frequently the foreign customers, contrary to popular myth, do not understand even basic English:

- 'We have problems with all languages. If a translator is not available then 'pidgin' English leads to chaos.' (Yorkshire and the Humber).
- 'Our Japanese agent speaks English but not as well as he thinks he does. Occasionally it would be useful to know what he is telling others during meetings.' (East of England).
- 'In Europe you can get by with only English, this is not true of China or Japan.' (East of England).

The customer may be young and have some English but a high-level capability in English should not be taken for granted; one North East England company reported difficulties in five markets partly due to the assumption that 'everyone speaks English':

- 'The Spanish don't mind speaking English but they generally can't!' (North West of England).
- 'Problems often occur not during sales but in after sales service and support. In these situations English is sometimes not spoken by the relevant persons.' (East of England).
- 'All our customers speak English but some do not speak it well and this leads to problems.' (East of England).
- 'A lot of our customers speak English but a lot still don't'. (Wales).
- 'France, Spain, Italy, Germany, the Netherlands – nobody available who speaks English.' (North East of England).

Language capability among Europeans

Yet how true is the widespread belief that all Europeans speak English? The most recent large-scale poll of language skills in the non-English native speaking European population remains the Eurobaromètre 54 Special Report, *Les Européens et les langues* (2001), which questioned 16,078 people in the EU (before the expansion into Eastern Europe) about their knowledge of languages.

In terms of the broad European population, the Eurobaromètre reports that 47% of Europeans speak only their mother tongue and no foreign language. Knowledge of English as a second language is highest among the Swedes (81%), the Dutch (80%) and the Danes (78%) and French is the most frequent foreign language spoken by the Irish (25%) and in the UK (22%). In terms of usage, English is the most frequently used foreign language (e.g. 70% in Sweden; 66% in Denmark). After English, German is the most used language in the Netherlands (28%) and in Denmark (18%). In terms of usefulness, English is seen by 75% of Europeans as the most useful; then French (40%), German (23%) and Spanish (18%). To summarise, the Danes, Swedes, and Dutch possess substantially greater linguistic capacity as nations than the Anglophone Irish and British populations.

When it comes to the industrial and commercial use of languages (see Appendix 1), it is clear that English remains by far the most widely used language in the European regions among companies where the three studies (ELUCIDATE, ELISE, REFLECT) were conducted. This view was further endorsed by the British Chambers of Commerce survey in 2004. In native English speaking territories, the pre-dominant foreign language is French. While English may be the predominant language in international business for most of these European companies, there is also significant use of French, German, Italian and Spanish as second languages; clear evidence of the importance of the use of other Scandinavian languages in Denmark; and small, but noticeable use of East Asian languages, such as Chinese and Japanese, in Scotland.

Moreover, many European companies lose business for lack of a range of languages. In the ELUCIDATE study (1999), for example, more Spanish companies (19%) claimed to have lost business than French (13%) or German (10%), while the percentage of companies facing language barriers is of a similar range to REFLECT – for example, southern German region (50%), western Spanish region (40%) and central France (35%). By comparison, in ELISE, the Dutch companies claim to be worst off (where 14% lose business), with all the other countries showing 6% or less. This probably has more to do with greater awareness among the Dutch of the role of languages, but also to the fact that they (like the British) trade extensively in faraway markets. No single European company, including the British, can be expected to have competence in all the languages of its actual or potential customers in the global marketplace and the most successful companies develop language strategies at company level, evidenced by linguistic competence among the employees themselves, to deal with this.

Why are there barriers with our nearest neighbour?

It is, paradoxically, the UK's nearest major export market, France, which poses significant barriers to many UK companies. English is not readily spoken: 'The French are particularly reluctant to speak English, particularly in France'. In this case, the East of England-based company seemed strangely surprised to discover that British companies trading in France were expected to use French!

Despite the widespread teaching of French in UK schools and the even greater spread of English in French schools, many language and cultural barriers with the French still exist; many UK companies report situations where communication with French trading partners has been problematic: 'acquisition of products' (West Midlands), 'specifications and negotiations' (West Midlands), negotiations and meetings (North East of England), 'purchasing spare parts' (North East of England), 'partnering/acting for buying and selling' (North East of England). 'Chasing payment' (West Midlands).

There seems to be a perception on the part of many British companies that there are both historical issues and a simple reluctance on the part of the French to speak English: '[We] would need French/Spanish to make progress with French manufacturers/customers ...' (West Midlands).

- 'In general English is well accepted other than in France.' (East of England)
- 'Very patriotic – people only speak in their language ...' (Yorkshire and the Humber)
- 'Even though the people could speak very good English they would not – hence we use translators.' (Yorkshire and the Humber)
- 'To use French in meetings, presentations and negotiations the speaker must be quite fluent. Otherwise French people get bored.' (East of England)

Do language barriers lead to lost business?

A significant minority of companies claim to have lost business as a direct result of language and/or cultural barriers. Companies tend to shy away from declarations of this type as they can imply some tangible business failing, or monetary loss, on the part of the company. The cost of lost business to the country as a consequence of international communication barriers is very difficult to measure where self-reporting is concerned, and even more so where respondents are diffident about admitting the full extent of the actual or potential losses. In many cases respondents recognise a failing but cannot accurately estimate the true cost. The extent of lost business is thought to be greater than most companies would estimate, though the basis for this argument is more qualitative than quantitative.

Just over a fifth of companies in the English and Welsh survey populations (21%), and a small but significant percentage of the Scottish and Northern Irish survey populations (6% and 14% respectively), acknowledge that they have directly lost business through language or cultural inadequacies. The highest regional figure is for the East of England (25%), followed by the North West (22%) and the West Midlands (22%). The lowest percentage declaring lost business (apart from Scotland, which had a low response rate) is for the North East (19%) and Wales (19%).

Other studies have produced different results based on different methodology. For example, in the Metra Martech study (1999) 7% of companies (representing all sizes of exporter – SME to large company – across all regions) indicated they had lost business, though the researchers add the comment: 'This is almost certainly an understatement of the real loss.'

In the *British Chambers of Commerce language survey* (2004) the figure is 4% (for companies losing business due to language barriers only, not including cultural obstacles) arising from misunderstanding orders, managing an agent or failing to answer telephone calls, but when giving these reasons company respondents do not make explicit reference to languages, so this finding is almost certainly an understatement.

Given that the LNTO/CILT figures are self-reported, it is likely that the percentage of companies actually losing business because of a lack of language skills is somewhere between 10% and 21%. Even if the lowest figure is extrapolated for all export companies in the UK, the potential loss of trade for the UK is significant.

Which situations lead to losses?

Figure 12 opposite gives a broad breakdown of the reasons perceived for losing international business. Many admissions of failure are captured in the catch-all 'inability to capitalise on opportunities' (23.4%).

The findings provide some specific insights into how companies can fail to capitalise on opportunities; a number do not follow up on enquiries from overseas (15% of mentions) and/or they lack the confidence either to operate in a foreign market or use a foreign language (12%). Lack of cultural empathy with potential foreign trading partners or clients ranks moderately high (10%), while problems with agents and distributors (10%) and problems at exhibitions and trade fairs (8%) offer some explanation as to the critical situations where, perhaps, most opportunities are lost.

There are four activities identified in the Metra Martech study (1999) which appear consistently to cause difficulties in about one third of exporting companies. Figure 13 opposite contains the percentage of companies declaring how well they are doing over the period 1996–1999. *Switchboard problems* (handling overseas callers) appear to pose major difficulties for 34% of companies, as do *preparing technical literature, negotiating contracts and agreements in a foreign language*. Even so, a majority apparently also rate their performance as either 'satisfactory' or 'good' for all three activities. What is surprising in the Metra Martech study (1999: 25) is that companies' own ratings of their performance in all these areas has generally been falling. However, this may be to do with increased awareness of the problem, rather than decreasing competence.

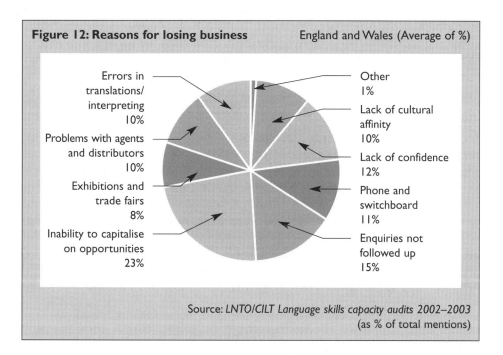

Figure 12: Reasons for losing business England and Wales (Average of %)

Errors in translations/ interpreting 10%

Problems with agents and distributors 10%

Exhibitions and trade fairs 8%

Inability to capitalise on opportunities 23%

Other 1%

Lack of cultural affinity 10%

Lack of confidence 12%

Phone and switchboard 11%

Enquiries not followed up 15%

Source: *LNTO/CILT Language skills capacity audits 2002–2003* (as % of total mentions)

Figure 13: Company ratings

	1996	1997	1999	1996	1997	1999	1996	1997	1999
Activity/Companies' own rating	Poor	Poor	Poor	Satis-factory	Satis-factory	Satis-factory	Good	Good	Good
Handling non-English speakers on the switchboard.	32%	33%	34%	38%	44%	41%	28%	21%	23%
Reading letters and faxes in a foreign language.	6%	19%	32%	23%	43%	37%	71%	39%	29%
Negotiating contracts and agreements in a foreign language.	2%	16%	34%	11%	25%	33%	86%	59%	31%
Preparing technical literature.	3%	19%	36%	9%	16%	35%	90%	88%	29%

Source: based on Metra Martech (1999: 25)

One comment by a company in the LNTO/CILT *East of England language skills capacity audit* seems particularly apposite in explaining the general uncertainty that surrounds how language capability can win orders abroad: they suspect that they had lost business with a prospective Spanish client but did not know the reason because of a lack of Spanish! 'With language we could perhaps have overcome the reason for losing the order' (East of England).

As we have seen in the *British Chambers of Commerce language survey* (2004), respondents rarely specify a lack of language skills as the main cause of failure. Companies frequently cite other reasons such as inappropriateness of their product rather than communication breakdown, thus identifying the symptom rather than the underlying cause. Respondents' comments give better insights into causes. They speak of telephone problems, difficulties for receptionists, misunderstandings over technical details and communicating with technical staff, difficulties following up initial interest and the general delays that come about from not having the language skills to hand to deal effectively with non-English speaking partners, clients or customers.

Earlier surveys have mentioned phone and switchboard-related problems as a major barrier and serve to confirm the critical importance of good communication at the first point of contact. From the Metra Martech study there is further confirmation that the ability to spontaneously react to a message or comment poses the greatest difficulty in most companies. Indeed, very few companies, particularly smaller ones, monitor the operation of their reception facility or switchboard. For example, it has been variously estimated that significant numbers of overseas calls in a foreign language can regularly get lost between the switchboard and the proposed recipient.

What solutions do companies find?

Many of the above failings could be addressed by adopting an international communication strategy underpinned by a set of quality procedures whereby 'opportunities' and 'enquiries' have to be followed up within a few working days in the appropriate language. Solutions, when they are implemented, can include using an on-line telephone interpreting service, or forwarding telephone and switchboard communications to a local language centre. A company keen to capture every opportunity can usually find some creative means of diverting calls to a friendly voice speaking the customer's language.

A recent National Languages for Export Regional Award winner has found that their attempt to sell medical equipment directly into France was not working. When they acquired a Paris telephone number from which they diverted calls to two French-speaking sales people in their UK office, sales suddenly increased dramatically.

Lacking language skills on site, many companies turn to external support for their international communication needs (see Figure 14 below).

Figure 14: The main uses and sources of external support		
Activity	**1997**	**1999**
Preparing literature	78%	60%
Negotiating contracts	70%	53%
Reading letters and faxes	46%	44%
Handling non-English speakers on the switchboard	16%	5%
Source		
Translation Agencies	65%	73%
Local Agents	43%	45%
Other	20%	19%

Source: based on Metra Martech (1999: 29)

Principal among these means of support are translation agencies and local agents. The Metra Martech study (1999) confirms that companies who leave all on trust to an English-speaking local agent tend to experience problems sooner or later. Sometimes, for example, the agent may be sourcing goods from several different suppliers despite an exclusivity agreement with the UK company. Moreover, companies are reliant on the agent's judgement of local market conditions and, if they do not speak the language, cannot check up themselves. Given that agents figure highly in the strategies cited by companies as a means of dealing with language barriers, it is a matter of concern that a local agent-cum-translator can be a double-edged sword. Many of the respondents feel that much could be improved by developing a better relationship with the local agent and being careful not to choose him or her purely on the basis of his or her ability to speak English. This means learning enough of the local language to manage the agent.

Some solutions can be as basic as learning just a few words of the customer's language as a matter of courtesy: 'All or most of our contacts speak fluent

English. The company has undertaken German language training as a courtesy.' (West Midlands).

Other companies take a series of practical steps, not only but also using local agents to handle language problems, but also employing language graduates, undertaking training or even seconding staff abroad to learn the local customs. In other cases, companies hope to get by on the strength of their product: 'They [the customers] laugh at us Brits speaking only English. We get by on the quality of our product. (But it puts us on the back foot.) (North West of England).

A good example of a case study of a company using an effective communication strategy is Ultraframe PLC (Clitheroe), North West England:

case study

Ultraframe PLC (Clitheroe), North West England

This company employs 1,300 people, has a turnover of £120 million and has been making conservatory roofs for fifteen years. It has recently bought out an American firm. The UK half of the firm does about £2 million worth of business in Europe at the moment. The intention is to grow the European business starting with France followed by Benelux. Expansion in Germany is delayed because there are problems with local standards to be resolved.

Using the customer's language is vital; 'The days of shouting at foreigners in English are long gone'. It is a matter of common courtesy as well as ability to compete. 'We are generally up against indigenous competitors so we have to go that extra mile to make ourselves more appealing'. They want to make it as easy as possible for foreign customers to deal with them even to the extent of arranging freephone numbers that do not indicate that the interlocutor (native speaker as far as possible) is in the UK.

They translate their literature in-house into French, German and Dutch consulting with customers or agents to get the terminology right. They do not much like translation agencies to which they would have to explain the technicalities of the business. They also supply graphics, photographs and text to their dealer customers for their own brochures.

They have an overseas sales department with five linguists, some of them bilingual or native speakers, covering French, Spanish and German competently and other languages at a basic level. They recruit people for their languages and will develop the above array as they target the Benelux countries.

They do have language and culture barriers. The current French agent is good but the Dutch one causes problems and 'not all Dutch people speak English in our industry'. They are also aware of differences of taste, lifestyle and legal requirements, etc – for example toughened glass is permitted in the UK but laminated glass is required elsewhere. However, the European Sales Manager declares that 'the main cultural barrier lies between the Export Department and the manufacturing side' (which does not easily accept the modifications that the foreign market needs).

Although the style of their products is not entirely suited to the French market and their prices are not the lowest, sales there have increased (from a low base) by 1,400% in a year.

Can the educational system help to alleviate barriers?

Rightly or wrongly, some UK exporters blame the school system for failing them, whereas others readily admit they did not take adequate advantage of the language facilities available to them during their years in formal education.

For the foreseeable future the number of British school leavers with language skills adaptable to their work environment will be limited. In the UK, and particularly in England, fewer than 10% of students aged 16+ continue studying a language as a main subject (Nuffield Inquiry Report 2000). So there is at present a diminishing prospect of UK companies finding enough speakers of foreign languages. The recently published report of the Tomlinson Working Group on 14–19 Reform makes a series of recommendations which may, in time, lead to a change for the better, but most professionals operating in the field accept that this will take at least a generation to achieve.

The regional variations in company language use suggest that there would be some justification for adapting the curriculum in secondary schools and colleges to include languages where there is significant regional or local demand. The more aware companies undertake their own training or introduce other strategies in the knowledge that the school system cannot reasonably ever quite match their specific and fast-changing market-led language needs.

The British Chambers research suggests there is a direct correlation between language competence and educational attainment. Their survey found that 75% of exporters with a bachelor's degree, or equivalent or higher qualification, speak a foreign language. This proportion falls to 62% for those holding A levels or equivalent and to just 50% for those with GCSEs/O levels, or lower level formal qualifications. French, followed by German, then Spanish are the languages most frequently found in each case.

In brief, a greater proportion of those who have attained a university degree or equivalent are able to speak a language more competently than those who simply attained GCSEs, equivalent or lower qualifications. Of these individual exporters, 29% educated to degree level claim to be so competent in a language that they can negotiate business deals. This proportion falls to 20% for those with A levels and just 9% for those with GCSEs or lesser qualifications. Export managers who studied languages at primary school claim to feel more confident in using a language. The conclusion is not necessarily that studying languages at primary level leads to successful exporting. It is likely that those who will become competent to conduct business in foreign languages are more likely to have had the opportunity for primary school education in a language and to have continued that learning throughout their formal education.

The corollary is that we should encourage more learning of languages from an early age and higher levels of general educational attainment in language relevant for the world of work.

Key points

There are many and varied reasons as to why companies can lose cross-border business. The communication dimension is present for many, but may or may not be identified as a primary cause depending on the company's level of awareness. There is a strong relationship between a company's level of pro-activity as an exporter and its recognition of the value of languages. The British Chambers of Commerce language survey (2004) gives an insight into the profile of companies that are more likely to use languages. Much has to do with the culture of the company and its attitude towards exporting, as well as the general educational attainment of its key personnel. Better educated staff in export companies tend to see the value of employing people with languages and in setting up international communication strategies. Of Enablers, 71% indicate that they consider it important to employ language skilled staff within their UK based offices, while the proportion falls to 56% for Adaptors, 40% for Developers and 30% for Opportunists. The economic value of the language and cultural component is fully recognised by Enablers but less so by the other groups who are more reactive in the exporting process.

The key challenge in helping companies to overcome international communication barriers has to be awareness-raising and enabling them to develop strategies so they think and operate more like Enablers or Adaptors. This significant shift of awareness is a key target for export advisory and support teams in and a declared objective for the CILT, the National Centre for Languages and its Regional Language Networks.

three

Cultural barriers

To what extent do companies face cultural barriers?

For a number of companies cultural barriers can be as significant an obstacle as languages. The average percentage for international companies in the UK facing cultural barriers in earlier studies is consistently 20% (Hagen 1999). In the more recent LNTO/CILT language skills audits the figure is also 20% for England and Wales; and in other studies 24% for Northern Ireland and 17% for Scotland. As with the figure for language barriers, these figures are likely to be an underestimation since identification of the source of the problem depends on high levels of awareness.

The Metra Martech study reports a higher percentage – 30% of UK exporting companies experienced a cultural barrier. While this finding is 10% higher than most other surveys have found, it still serves to highlight a growing problem for international trading companies.

Cultural difficulties are frequently referred to in detail in the case studies of the LNTO/CILT language skills audits. They include differences in generic patterns of behaviour in everyday life, for example, concept of time; body language; meals and eating; trust and respect; religious beliefs; and social habits. Differences in business practice are also identified as an issue, for example, specification and presentation of detail; style and content of sales materials; invoicing and chasing payment; credit and delivery terms; methods of reaching the market. Cultural differences are a significant factor in successful marketing: understanding customer preferences, such as colours, size of packaging and even typeface can make a difference between success and failure.

In this complex minefield of 'differentness' companies are only sometimes aware of occasions where they have given offence. For example, one company recognised it had upset its Greek customers by declining to stay for lunch. Offence can be taken by either party. The manager of a Welsh company found the Japanese behaviour 'so bizarre' ('compared to the Taiwanese, Chinese and Koreans') that he gave up trying to do business with them. Others considered some cultural issues trivial: '[we are] not impressed by stories of offending the Indians by wearing leather shoes' (Wales).

Which markets give rise to cultural barriers?

Companies facing cultural barriers cite Japan as trickiest (16%), followed by France (12%), the Middle East (12%), China (11%) and Germany (9%) (see Figure 15 opposite). Despite the frequency of company mentions of French language skills, France is also the most frequently mentioned European market giving rise to cultural barriers. For this reason, a special section has been devoted later in this chapter to exploring cultural barriers to trading with France.

It is sometimes said that there are no real cultural barriers in Europe. Yet cultural barriers for trade with France, Germany, Spain and Italy are placed high on the list, perhaps inevitably in view of the greater frequency of business in those markets compared with the more distant ones. There is a rough 50:50 split between cultural barriers in trade with European and non-European markets. The picture has changed little over the last five years. In 1999 Japan was already considered the most problematic country (with 20% of all mentions), followed by the Middle East (14%) and China (10%). Fewer respondents are claiming to have met cultural obstacles in trading with France ((10%), it is always possible that this is due to a lack of awareness of the obstacles.

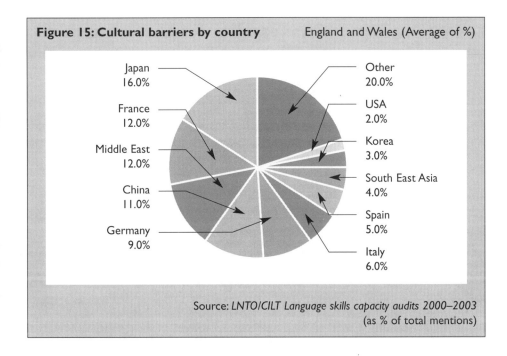

Figure 15: Cultural barriers by country   England and Wales (Average of %)

Japan
16.0%

France
12.0%

Middle East
12.0%

China
11.0%

Germany
9.0%

Other
20.0%

USA
2.0%

Korea
3.0%

South East Asia
4.0%

Spain
5.0%

Italy
6.0%

Source: *LNTO/CILT Language skills capacity audits 2000–2003*
(as % of total mentions)

Other regional variations exist: for example, in the West Midlands, Germany is considered as culturally problematical as Japan and in the South West, France and Germany are both in the top five. Only North East companies have experienced a greater proportion of cultural problems in the Middle East and Asia compared with the countries of Europe. The picture for Scotland, Wales and Northern Ireland is quite similar: Japan, China and the Middle East again represent the top non-European countries posing cultural barriers.

In which situations do cultural barriers most arise?

The range of situations where cultural differences are experienced are generally either very culture-specific, suggesting that greater awareness of the local business environment is required, or generic, suggesting that some awareness concerning 'etiquette' in the broadest sense would be helpful. The occasions where cultural barriers occur are shown schematically in Figure 16 overleaf. **Business etiquette**, **management style**, **meetings** and **social behaviour** are the most oft-quoted generic categories posing problems. Etiquette is a multi-faceted concept. One issue of etiquette was raised by a company in the context of a problem with the Dutch who are commonly supposed to have similar cultural values and behaviour to the English: 'Issues of hierarchy, meeting etiquette, gift giving, kissing or not kissing'.

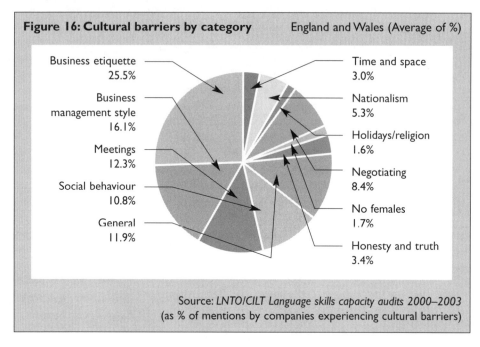

Figure 16: Cultural barriers by category   England and Wales (Average of %)

Business etiquette 25.5%
Business management style 16.1%
Meetings 12.3%
Social behaviour 10.8%
General 11.9%
Time and space 3.0%
Nationalism 5.3%
Holidays/religion 1.6%
Negotiating 8.4%
No females 1.7%
Honesty and truth 3.4%

Source: *LNTO/CILT Language skills capacity audits 2000–2003*
(as % of mentions by companies experiencing cultural barriers)

Quotations from respondents and personal accounts offer the greatest insight into the detail of how specific cultures differ. In the ELUCIDATE study the same issues were raised: business etiquette (35%) was again most frequently cited, followed by social behaviour – entertaining, social customs, humour, etc – (12%) and management style (11%).

Do other European companies face similar barriers?

Figure 26 in Appendix 1 shows which parts of the world give rise to cultural obstacles for the European companies surveyed. The region most likely to cause cultural barriers for companies in England/Wales, Portugal, Northern Ireland, Scotland and the Netherlands is East Asia; where Japan and China are most often cited.

Trade with the Middle East poses cultural barriers, particularly for Danish and Scottish companies. Cultural problems are also posed in trading with France, particularly for English, Welsh, Polish, Irish and Dutch companies. Germany poses obstacles for the Polish, Irish and Dutch. The causes are many and varied, encompassing a wide range of societal, behavioural and interpersonal differences, but they are often caused by a general lack of awareness and cultural sensitivity.

Qualitative data provides a much clearer picture of issues concerned here. Quotations from companies show that business relationships can give rise to communication difficulties ranging from the consequence of an alternative view of the world or just a misunderstanding of words.

Cultural obstacles are very diverse and are often linked to language difficulties. Cultural obstacles are widespread and not restricted to English or Welsh companies, i.e. those with the most limited access to in-house language skills. This is also apparent from comments made during the REFLECT study:

- 'Brazil has Portuguese as its language, but a completely different business culture.' (Portuguese company)
- 'We lack knowledge of the culture of selling, particularly in non-European countries.' (Irish company)
- 'It is difficult to penetrate Japanese companies due to "outsider" status.' (English company)

The most significant reasons given are: 'lack of confidence', 'inability to capitalise on opportunities' or 'inability to negotiate'. The quotations from individual employees do not necessarily represent their respective company's policy or attitude towards a particular culture or country. Comments exemplify (i) the level of often naive understanding of foreign cultures; and (ii) the broad range of cultural diversity that companies have to deal with (and for which many are ill-equipped). The comments can also reveal as much about the individual's own perceptions, or prejudice, as about any real obstacles.

- 'In Germany if you can prove that what you've got is better than what they've got, they'll buy it.' (Wales)
- 'Need for much greater relationship-building [in Italy].' (East of England)
- 'English often too polite and don't get the same success rate within Germanic cultures, as they don't insist enough.' (East of England)
- 'Total lack of understanding of punctuality by them [Indonesians].' (West Midlands)
- 'We did not appreciate the 'getting to know you' culture before going in for the hard sell [in the Pacific Rim].' (West Midlands)
- 'You need to respect the very long history of China.' (South West of England)

Is there a relationship between culture and language?

Cultural issues can frequently arise in dealings with Northern Americans, including Canadians despite the common language. They can also arise with traditional speakers of English as a second language such as Indians and Pakistanis. Despite superficial impressions of cultural and linguistic homogeneity, countries like the Netherlands and Sweden can also pose significant cultural barriers: e.g. in the Netherlands: '[We've problems in] business negotiation and understanding real intentions', or Sweden: where there are complaints about 'Lack of leadership' (East of England). In the USA there is the 'tendency to exaggerate, business policy, negotiation style' (East of England). Such remarks exemplify the adage of 'two nations divided by a common language'. The rationale for cultural awareness training, and at the least awareness-raising programmes, is very strong and applies for companies trading in all markets, English-speaking, as well as non English-speaking.

Barriers in Europe

France

The French market presents significant linguistic as well as cultural challenges, which can arise, in particular, as a consequence of traditional Anglo-French mistrust. The French are perceived not to wish to speak English. 'French customers are less keen than others to speak English, though they can' and 'the French never speak English and it's won't rather than can't'.

• 'It's essential to speak French in France.' (Wales)

One Welsh company employee endeavoured to pinpoint more accurately a cultural mismatch:

• 'Too many artificial barriers and a complete refusal to [make] agreements and timetables make this closed market very unattractive.' (Wales)

Other issues raised are lack of compatibility of software, working patterns and structures and different approaches to technology applications and tendering processes.

Germany and Switzerland

Germany seems to pose general interpersonal miscommunication problems:

• 'Difficult to gauge reactions.' (East of England)

Issues of 'inflexibility' and 'not [being] open to ideas that are not German (the 'not invented here' syndrome)', the 'importance of detail' are raised, as well as expectations of quality:

- 'Cultural expectations of contracts, performance, quality.' (West Midlands).
- '[In Germany they are] less prepared to accept technical data/results from non-German sources.' (Wales).

There are observations on the German manner, which again, may, however, reveal more about the assumptions and expectations of the survey respondents than about Germans.

- 'Germans appear more forceful than one finds in the UK.' (West Midlands).
- 'Some countries [Germany] can be more demanding than others ... they are sticklers.' (South West of England).

One company that has encountered and learned to overcome cultural barriers is Doyen Medipharm Ltd (Barton).

case study

Doyen Medipharm Ltd (Barton), East of England

Interview with the Sales Director of Doyen Medipharm Ltd in Barton, Cambridgeshire, a medium-sized company with 45 staff and a turnover of £3 million. They have an American sister company and a Malaysian subsidiary. They export 50% of their packaging machinery (costing from £100k to £700k) mainly to Europe.

Languages are important to the company, from employing people with languages to having a website in English and German (soon French also). They do not, however, have many linguists (about four in all) with levels of skill from basic to fluent in French and German. They do not employ agents, 'we've tried agents and it has never worked', because of their technically sophisticated machinery and long development times. They therefore rely to a large extent on customers speaking English.

They have encountered cultural barriers, for example 'the French and the English have an adversarial relationship'. 'The Germans are a lot more straightforward as long as you can persuade them that they are buying the best product.' The Scandinavians are easy to do business with. They do a little business with Portugal where 'there is no reluctance but a slight language barrier since not everyone speaks English'. 'The Finns are very nice to deal with, the professionals speak good English.' 'There are cultural things in Malaysia but we employ locals who can deal with them.'

With their EU customers (most of their business) there are few problems relating to procedures or business practice, except that some customers require a bank guarantee in return for the substantial deposit with order that Doyen requires. They have not undertaken any training in language or culture although language skill is a criterion for employment in some positions and their Sales Manager has lived and worked in Germany and France. They do use translators regularly and there was one recent 'disaster when an agency that they had used before produced a bad translation of a machinery manual – as the customer quickly pointed out: 'the words are Finnish but we cannot understand the text'.

Source: LNTO/CILT East of England language skills capacity audit

Other European countries

Trading with other European cultures can create a completely different set of obstacles for UK companies. Many remark on issues of poor timekeeping in other parts of Europe and complain about: 'flexible time, deadlines and (poor) punctuality' in Italy and Greece, again revealing expectations rooted in UK business practice and a lack of awareness about practice elsewhere.

Some remark on what they perceive as 'the innate suspiciousness' of the accession countries in Eastern Europe, which in some cases are still struggling to shed the strictures of their recent past. Other comments suggest that cultural problems often arise as a consequence of traditionally heavier-handed bureaucracies: 'In Poland expect big delays – documents get lost and paperwork has to be re-done.' 'Czech paperwork is horrendous – if they don't understand what something is they quarantine it!' Not unexpectedly, cultural barriers are perceived to be even more widespread the further from their domestic market that companies trade; the Middle East, Latin America and, in particular, East Asia, pose more noticeable difficulties.

Barriers in East Asia

East Asia is the region that gives rise to most comment. Companies regard these markets as places where 'it is very easy to make cultural gaffes ... it is easy to make a faux pas, for example because those cultures (Japanese and Korean) are so hierarchical' (North West of England). This is due not only to outward variations in taste, symbol, behaviour and manner, but there are fundamental differences of philosophy, such as Confucianism with its tendency towards long-term thinking and planning, which are fundamental to understanding the mindset of the trading partner.

Companies find Japanese business 'slow' (North East of England) and Japanese negotiating can easily 'lead to misunderstandings' ... it is possible to misunderstand 'the fluid nature of Japanese negotiating.' (East of England).

Companies remark on the tendency of the Japanese to prefer to buy from their compatriots, as do the Germans, French and many other trading nations with a strong manufacturing base. One company observes that etiquette requires people not to speak 'out of turn'. 'There are very specific ways to work and deal with the Japanese in business and special rules to follow: it is important to deal with those with authority, which makes life much easier.'

There is a different emphasis in China and it is clear that some companies have learned to appreciate that, while there are common characteristics in East Asian societies, there are also many more differences. The Chinese image of inscrutability is raised and 'you can get little feedback'. East of England companies have found that 'tendering procedures (are problematical)', 'the Chinese make decisions by committee', Chinese people must not lose face in any way: 'you must flatter them and stay calm' and 'wait for a consensus in China'.

For the Chinese, silence is also a powerful communication tool and 'you need an expert in the language and the culture to indicate the banana skins'.

A list follows of some of the more common cultural differences that UK companies have discovered in trading in the Far East, which are substantiated in the work of Tung (1996) and Gesteland (2003):

• The importance of guanxi (connections or contacts).
• The importance of not losing face and of saving your interlocutor's face.
• An acceptance of the Taoist belief – 'cyclical movement': everything occurs in cycles. So people should be modest in their success.
• The family, the nation and the company are considered more important than the individual, especially in China, Hong Kong and Taiwan).
• The importance of hard work, thrift, hierarchy and perseverance.
• Recognition of the inherent contradictions of life (including the female-male dichotomy of yin and yang).

This means that in general these countries prefer a team-based approach, with a hierarchical model of organisation.

A need to indulge in strategies or mind games to expose any hidden meanings in communications.

The impact on business is:

• The team's or group's happiness and harmony are more valuable than individual success.
• Younger people should show respect towards the older, more senior people.
• The boss has very high status and is likely to make more of the decisions.

To be successful at crossing cultural boundaries, creating a personal relationship can be paramount. This case study from the South West of England shows a developing sophistication in preparing for and dealing with cultural differences, and building the personal relationship, all of which underpin successful trading with any other country.

Pal Media Services, South West England

Pal Media is a small company that creates and publishes multimedia products, makes TV documentary material and runs a language school for foreign students, established 27 years ago. They export 60% of their products.

They do not encounter language barriers and the only cultural barrier mentioned is when dealing with the Japanese. 'They do business in a very different way. Their body language is different. It is difficult to know whether you are scoring points. We get people to help us and ask them to interpret the messages.'

Europeans are seen as fairly straightforward 'as long as you have some party skills, especially the Latins.' 'People like you to be a person first and a businessman second', to go for a drink or a meal and talk about the family.

Source: *LNTO/CILT South West of England Regional Development Agency language skills capacity audit*

Barriers in the Middle East

Companies trading with the Middle East face different kinds of cultural issues: the personal dimension of dealing with a person means understanding family relations and often meeting members of his or her family. Religion can be another source of different cultural difference and many UK companies are well aware of the need to take account of carefully observed religious holidays and feasts, as well as respect for holy shrines.

Employing women on business assignments in the Middle East can pose a serious problem for western companies operating in the local culture: 'Problems for female sales staff – we used males as this circumvented difficulties' (Scotland); even 'discrimination against women'(Northern Ireland). 'The obvious [cultural problems] exist. In certain markets you cannot send a woman; e.g. the Middle East and Indonesia' (South West of England). Similarly, in the LNTO/CILT East of England language skills capacity audit 'dealing with women is a problem ... they prefer not to.'

Time is not a uniform cultural concept – 'the length of time to make decisions', 'timekeeping' and 'observing meeting arrangements' are very different from those with which UK companies are familiar. 'There is a need to understand culture and values – in most cases the way of doing business is very different and will take more time to build a relationship' (Wales).

Language knowledge does not automatically lead to cultural knowledge. Each culture is unique, multi-faceted and constantly changing and it appears that the foundation for success lies in recognising this and one's own preconceptions, respecting differences and learning either to work with, or around, the differences.

Key points

Cultural awareness training is a major solution for many companies. Having 'cultural sensitivity' makes it possible to learn to work with, or around, the differences. In the LNTO/CILT *East of England language skills capacity audit* an International Trade Adviser seems to state the underlying truth: 'You need to play their game in order to build a relationship'.

As a minimum, many companies have gained from developing a better awareness of their own cultural norms and a greater sensitivity and respect for 'otherness', which can simply mean being 'polite and sensitive to what people tell you' (Wales). 'No one should leave these shores (try to enter a foreign market) without a cultural briefing' (North West Business Link Manager).

Companies, even if they cannot make full use of languages, need to do their cultural preparation homework, before setting out. According to an International Trade Adviser quoted in the LNTO/CILT *North West of England language skills capacity audit* (2003), 'Cultural awareness may be more important than language skills and everyone can learn the cultural aspect: how business is done, how people are, etc.' It is clear from the surveys that there is a wide range of areas of cultural differences that could be addressed through a series of measures: consultation with experts, employing agents. While a short briefing on etiquette can help to avoid serious faux pas, often a more extensive training programme is necessary.

The rationale for incorporating cultural awareness as part of a company's international communication strategy is very powerful and applies to all markets, English-speaking (e.g. USA, Australia), as well as non English-speaking.

four

The importance of international communication strategies

The winning companies in the UK's National Languages for Export Award Scheme have demonstrated that an international communication, or language, strategy, has enabled them to be more effective at overcoming language and cultural barriers. One finding of the Metra Martech (1999) study is that companies are becoming more aware of the need for an international communication strategy. However, few have yet moved to the implementation stage. For example, it is reported that 44% of a sample of exporters had 'noticed' articles about language issues in 1999 and were more aware of the issues, compared with only 41% of the same sample in 1997 (Metra Martech 1999), but many were still unable to translate this into action: 'Language strategy sounds such a difficult piece of work and we really struggle to promote language audits for example.' (Chamber Business Enterprises, Manchester Chamber of Commerce, North West of England).

What is an international communication strategy?

An international communication strategy is a set of integrated mechanisms for dealing with predictable language and cultural problems before they arise and having in place recognised tactics for coping also with the unexpected. Many companies wrongly interpret 'international communication strategy' as last-minute preparation taken to mitigate any obvious language or cultural problem, like the cultural content of the overseas mission pre-briefing meeting, or even listening to a cultural briefing cassette on the way to the airport.

A company-wide international communication strategy comprises a number of measures, such as responding in the customer's language, translating company sales and trade literature, employing native speakers (with cultural as well as linguistic skill), using websites, paying for language training and recruiting staff with language knowledge. Some of these are difficult to implement for a variety of reasons: suitable native speakers with business skills may not be easy to find, as are school leavers or university graduates with relevant language knowledge and business skills, and training in small companies can be expensive, time-consuming and sometimes ineffective, so the costs can outweigh the benefits. But the systematic introduction of an international communication strategy is a powerful solution.

The holistic strategic approach of an international communications strategy goes much deeper and involves integrating a number of different approaches into a single approach: combining an international human resource development strategy by setting up continuous training, or the recruitment of native speakers or graduate linguists, or developing a multilingual document management system. The common thread is that the strategy offers a quality plan that pre-empts potential barriers by putting procedures in place for dealing with them ahead of time. A company with a known set of procedures and planned capacity, whether in-house or outsourced, is less likely to be caught out by language and cultural barriers and can respond quickly to a foreign sales lead, or an early joint venture approach when it comes through. So the company builds up language and culture capacity at all stages of the process: from product development, packaging and delivery to after-sales service.

How can a strategy help?

There are particular interfaces of contact with overseas customers where good communication is vital, namely:

- **Sales and marketing**: i.e. dealing with direct sales, organising translation of communications, contracts and promotional literature.
- **Secretarial/administration**: i.e. communications in another language can be handled quickly and efficiently from the start.
- **Product and packaging design**: when colours, symbols, gesticulations and names on packaging can mean entirely different things in different countries.

It is also vital in a group of written communications where good translation is essential:

- incoming and outgoing correspondence, fax, memos, invoices, e-mail;
- company documents, reports, product and technical information, financial reports, accounts;
- literature, advertising material;
- contracts, legal rules, regulations, patents and local standards;
- instructions, manuals, procedures and specifications.

Use of the appropriate language can greatly improve all areas of spoken communication, whether undertaken directly by company employees or through an interpreter. Some obvious instances are:

- formal, informal and social meetings with foreign customers and colleagues;
- telephone calls, involving sales or enquiries, technical support;
- negotiating; videoconferencing; travelling;
- public presentations, speeches, or language use at seminars, conferences, exhibitions;
- and of course, at reception, at the switchboard – the first point of contact for many companies in the UK.

What does a good international communication strategy look like?

Many companies ask this question. Ideally it means:

- communications received in a foreign language, such as a phone-call, e-mail or letter, are dealt with promptly by an individual trained to respond in the right language;
- staff can sort foreign communications into 'urgent' and 'non-urgent' and pass them on to the right person;
- professional interpreters and translators are known, and know the company well, and can be brought in quickly at critical times;
- knowledge of the customer's language and culture informs the export strategy;
- potential foreign language and culture pitfalls are spotted in advance and tactics for dealing with these incorporated into planning.

Examples

'Best practice' companies featured in the survey case studies adopt a wide range of international export communication measures to solve their problems:

- using inexpensive software to understand the gist of an e-mail;
- hiring a chauffeur-cum-translator via the embassy;

- grouping linguists in the Overseas Sales Department (a larger company);
- recruiting foreign nationals and employing language professionals for specific tasks;
- planning a long term languages strategy (rarely found among the companies surveyed);
- employing agents with good English;
- 'piggy-backing' on the language facilities of a partner company;
- studying the foreign culture in advance of going abroad to avoid the more obvious faux pas.

How many companies have a strategy?

In the LNTO/CILT language skills audits companies were asked if they had a formal international communication, or language, strategy and only 11% of the aggregate of the English and Welsh samples claimed to have one. So only about one in ten knowingly have one. There are, however, regional and national variations: at the two extremes this ranged from 14% in the West Midlands to 9% in Yorkshire and the Humber, South West of England, and Wales.

In the European surveys, by comparison, nearly half of the companies in Poland, Portugal, Denmark and about a third of companies in the Netherlands claim to have a language strategy in place. This compares sharply with Scotland (5%), England and Wales (11%) and Northern Ireland, Sweden and Germany (all 12%). The lack of a language strategy in the majority of the English-speaking companies may help to explain the high proportion of those companies claiming to experience language barriers.

Where an international communications strategy does exist, as in Datum Alloys, they exert a very positive effect on the company's trading position.

case study

DATUM ALLOYS (Kingsbridge), South West England

An exporter of Metals and Alloys, employing twenty people, trading for seven years and with a turnover of £2 million. The company imports 50% of its raw material from very large US metal concerns and exports 60% of its product mainly to European countries.

The main languages are German, French, Italian and Dutch. The company considers languages to be very important and using the customer's own language is part of a 'quality service'.

Part of their policy is to employ foreign nationals in their own countries, as employees not agents. They consider this to be viable and measure the employee's cost-effectiveness by the quantity of sales they bring in. They also need linguists in the office to respond to queries. ('The Dutch are a bit more willing to speak English than some others so we could try ringing up a Dutch customer in English.')

They do not think that they have encountered language or culture barriers that have resulted in lost business. 'If there is a problem the local representative (employee) will visit the customer.'

They invest in language training using private trainers and one objective may be to 'tweak conversational French or German for a business context'. They have not used local colleges but would do so depending on the quality of training offered.

Translation has been bought in particularly for the contracts of foreign nationals employed by the company in their own countries.

They are sure that their languages policy has been successful. 'We do not like to force customers into speaking English.' 'The product is technical and we wish to avoid errors.' 'If you wish to make sales into Europe you have to put in the investment to get the results.'

Source: LNTO/CILT South West of England language skills capacity audit

---

It is clear that many companies do not fully understand the notion of what an international communication strategy comprises. This may be a simple issue of semantics, some respondents denied having a strategy, but, when questioned more closely, revealed they had an array of measures embedded in their export planning which suggested they had unconsciously developed a strategy as a form of good practice. Measures like using local agents to help minimise language problems, responding in the customer's language, adapting websites to the customer's language and culture, or employing foreign nationals, and so on, can form an effective strategy for a number of companies. However, having only one element from the array would be too limited to merit designation as a 'strategy'. In fact, the features of 'Opportunists' and 'Developers' in the *British Chambers of Commerce language survey* (2004) suggest that relying on agents or distributors alone for international communication solutions does not necessarily lead to high growth exports.

Figure 17 opposite provides an overview of the various elements that usually comprise an international communication strategy. The list is based on respondents declaring evidence of a strategic element or strand integrated into their planning. The commonest strand in a language strategy is using local agents to solve language problems, though several companies refer to a heavy over-reliance on local agents as a potential problem:

• 'We have agents in all the countries in which we operate.' (Wales)
• 'Agents speak the local language plus English. We keep to English for all correspondence and quotations, etc.' (Wales)

Agents frequently act as translators, interpreters and advisers for all types of international communication problems, but as mentioned previously this is not without its risks. Problems with managing local agents can itself lead to lost business.

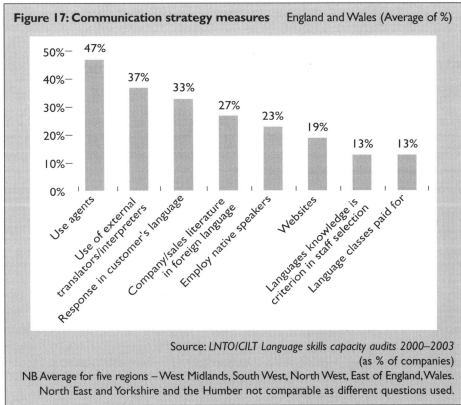

Figure 17: Communication strategy measures   England and Wales (Average of %)

Source: *LNTO/CILT Language skills capacity audits 2000–2003*
(as % of companies)
NB Average for five regions – West Midlands, South West, North West, East of England, Wales.
North East and Yorkshire and the Humber not comparable as different questions used.

In the 1999 Metra Martech study respondents were asked to indicate how they overcame language problems in non-English speaking markets. The responses largely matched the later LNTO/CILT language skills audits' finding – that there were three key tactics for overcoming barriers (Figure 18).

Figure 18: Tactics for overcoming barriers

Strategy	Positive responses (n=503)
Local agents	70%
Hire of overseas staff	40%
Translation companies	34%

The commentary emphasised the value of agents but only as a first step: 'The use of local agents is a typical first export route, but it side-steps the language and cultural problems and is not necessarily the most effective way of exporting in the long term' (Metra Martech, 1999). One cautionary remark was also made about agents by a Welsh company who said, '[they] have a different agenda to yours'.

Success through an international communication strategy

In samples of companies which have the greatest language problems, there is not surprisingly less evidence of international communication strategies. This is for a variety of reasons, but often the main one is the unquestioned assumption that people abroad will always speak English.

There are other factors to bear in mind. The evidence also seems to show that companies are more likely to have an international communication strategy as their size increases (up to 500 employees), as their turnover increases and as the proportion of their product exported increases (up to 50%). In other words, larger companies are more likely to implement an international communication strategy.

One of the most significant findings in the ELUCIDATE study was an inter-relationship between companies' development of language strategies and a lower incidence of language barriers. This finding is also confirmed in the ELISE study: perhaps not altogether unsurprisingly, companies which have thought through the language and cultural issues and developed solutions appear not to encounter as many barriers. The surprise is that such beneficial and enlightened practice is not more widespread.

From the *British Chambers of Commerce language survey* (2004) it is apparent that groups of Adaptors and Enablers are most likely to incorporate the elements of a language strategy within their export strategy. The Enablers, who account for 20% of SME exporters in the British Chambers of Commerce sample, epitomise the international communication strategy approach and are 'characterised by their proactive export approach, consciously choosing markets where they want a presence, adapting and localising their products, services and sales literature and placing considerable importance on their UK based staff having foreign language skills'.

In other words the tactics referred to are simply the instruments of the strategy; the translating, recruitment and training are the means to successful exporting. Other companies do not have the skills on site and require external support. However, it would appear that professional translators are a resource that is often undervalued and under-used by British companies. More companies need to recognise when they have a need for professional intervention and need to have, as part of their exporting plan, access to language and cultural resources and local facilities: a local translation agency, a training company, a local college or university language centre, a BLIS Professionals listed trainer, even a tailored open-learning programme

More importantly, the British Chambers findings confirm that the 'higher the export turnover the greater the importance is placed on employment of staff with language skills in the UK.' Of exporters responsible for an annual export turnover in excess of £5 million 69% indicate these skills are important compared, at the other extreme, to just 28% of those responsible for a turnover of £100k or less.

It is apparent that a fundamental prerequisite to an effective international communication strategy is the company's predisposition to, and an in-company culture of, adaptability and a proactive responsiveness to overseas market conditions, including local culture and language.

Some of the comments in the LNTO/CILT language skills audits confirm the existence of a respect for language competence among proactive export companies which fits with the profile of the British Chambers of Commerce's Enabler group. There are, for example, the views of Welsh companies who, with their general willingness to be 'user friendly', declare: 'it is a matter of pride' [to communicate in the customer's language]; 'just [having] English is off-putting'; 'languages are vital to function in Europe and it is very arrogant to expect other people always to speak English' and 'if you can't communicate with the customer you can't do business'. (Wales).

As a rule of thumb, companies with the best practice in this area employ most of the elements that make up an international communication strategy, such as the Enablers and to a lesser extent the Adaptors of the British Chambers of Commerce language survey (2004). The lower percentage for companies 'responding in the customer's language', as revealed in the LNTO/CILT language skills audits is a matter for concern, but fits with the characteristics of the Developers who tend to favour approaches from distributors and agents. Similarly, not just translating but also adapting the company website for an overseas customer is a key feature of advanced company practice. Few Opportunists and Developers produce a foreign language literature or a website adapted for their customers abroad (see Figure 19).

Figure 19: Tactics for overcoming barriers

	Opportunists	Developers	Adaptors	Enablers
Adapted product	31%	72%	78%	85%
Adapted literature	19%	21%	84%	92%
Adapted website	11%	8%	24%	31%
(No website)	19%	12%	8%	7%

Source: *British Chambers of Commerce language survey* (2004)

Companies are being increasingly categorised into 'language-aware' and 'language-unaware' based on their level of awareness and use of the customer's language. Enablers and Adaptors (with strategies) tend to fall into the first category and Developers and Opportunists into the second.

The Anglocentric comments made by companies which have an international communication strategy are quite distinct from those who do not. This becomes very apparent in the LNTO/CILT North West of England language skills capacity audit when the views of language-aware companies are compared with those of language-unaware ones.

Comments of North West of England companies **without** an international communication strategy:

- 'Most customers speak fluent English.'
- '[We] rely on customers and suppliers to speak and write English.'
- 'We are using the English language skills of our partners mostly.'
- 'English has become [an] internationally accepted form of communication.'
- 'We use the international business language, English.'
- 'I am in the business of making money not learning languages.'
- 'If we need to send a letter we use a piece of translation software costing £50.'

Comments from North West of England companies **with** an international communication strategy:

- 'We can speak German, French, Italian and Portuguese.'
- 'We employ a German interface on a part-time basis in Germany.'
- 'We recruit language-capable staff.'
- 'We are unique in employing entirely foreign operations staff.'
- 'The days of shouting at foreigners in English are long gone. We are generally up against indigenous competitors so we have to go that extra mile [and use local languages].'
- 'We use languages simply, to open a door, to get from a receptionist to an English speaker, to send a quote if it would be received better in the local language, etc.'
- 'The Germans appreciate your making an effort to speak German (even if you are not very good).'
- 'They laugh at us Brits speaking only English. It may be good-natured but it puts us on the back foot.'
- 'It [languages] is becoming more of an issue rather than less.'

Most companies with an international communication strategy, such as Enablers and Adaptors, also tend to employ staff with good language skills or native speakers for a range of business purposes, such as:

- producing sales literature, legal, scientific or technical documents (or shipping documents);

- helping with local presentations;
- producing instruction materials;
- helping at exhibition stands.

Training is also a principal feature or measure of an international communication strategy, yet surprisingly few companies seem to take it up.

Language training as a strategy measure

Only about a quarter (23%) of the English and Welsh companies surveyed by LNTO/CILT indicated they had taken up language training in the previous three years. This is similar to the Metra Martech (1999) findings, in which 24% of companies had invested in professional language training or taken language classes in the previous eighteen months.

Many exporters recognise the impracticality of learning languages on a tight timescale, with a small budget and in a world in which the decision about which language to learn is not always immediately obvious.

One company, which responded to the *British Chambers of Commerce language survey* (2004), observes: 'How many languages can you learn? Cultural studies might be better, so you can learn historical and cultural values of a country, which allows you to market to them better.'

The languages in which training has taken place, from the evidence of LNTO/CILT language skills audits respondents are shown in Figure 20 overleaf. German, French, Spanish and Italian are again the top four, and Russian, Chinese and Japanese feature. Training in Russian has risen ahead of Chinese and Japanese, compared with earlier surveys, which may reflect increasing opportunities in Eastern Europe, for example, with the opening up of Russia and the former Soviet Union.

There are also regional variations in the take-up of language training.

	Chinese	Japanese	Russian
National average	2%	3%	3%
South West			6%
North East		6%	
North West	7%	5%	
East	4%		

Most individuals are being trained either at evening classes or during the day, usually on release. Self-tuition is higher than expected, but this may be explained by the attraction of time flexibility and the increasing availability of higher quality training materials and programmes, both on- and off-line.

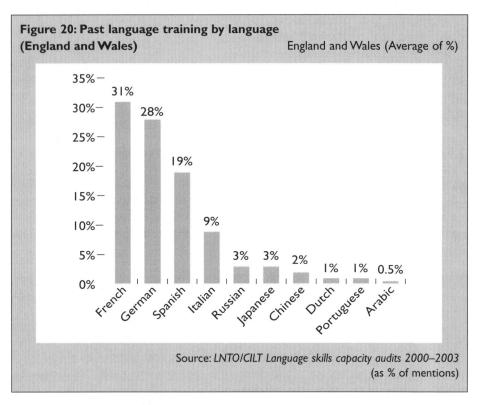

Figure 20: Past language training by language (England and Wales)
England and Wales (Average of %)

Source: LNTO/CILT Language skills capacity audits 2000–2003
(as % of mentions)

One example of strategic practice is that of an employer in the North West of England, who already has significant language skills among his employees as a consequence of a recruitment policy favouring people with language skills. The

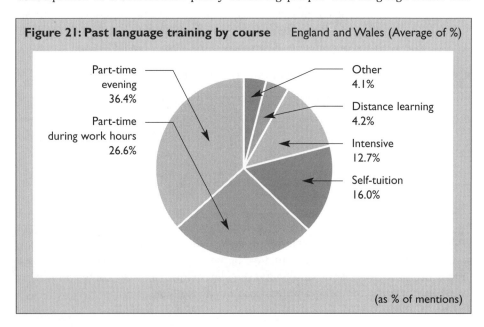

Figure 21: Past language training by course
England and Wales (Average of %)

Part-time evening 36.4%

Part-time during work hours 26.6%

Other 4.1%

Distance learning 4.2%

Intensive 12.7%

Self-tuition 16.0%

(as % of mentions)

employer will also pay for extra language training if it is useful to the company. This approach is contrasted with companies which may install an open learning centre offering 'popular' German and Spanish classes of a 'holiday/introduction to' type of a general nature and quite unrelated to any explicit company needs or strategy.

Opinions expressed by respondent companies in the North West of England are fairly typical of employer attitudes towards language training: fewer than half (44.9%) of the small number of North West companies who had undertaken training believed that it had been successful and/or contributed to improved business performance. One North West company was atypical in requiring its language training to have 'relevance and flexibility' and very effectively opted for integrating several schemes; namely, an (expensive) intensive course followed by a six-month placement, as well as a holiday-orientated evening class. .

The case studies are full of approval for language skills in principle. Companies have found a range of solutions, such as using a software translation package; concentrating linguists in their Sales Department; employing foreign nationals; and training. Among self-help measures to be taken by exporting companies, the least likely option is usually language training, because it requires the most time commitment and highest investment.

- 'I can understand the smaller companies' reluctance to train in languages with their limited resources and time.' (North West of England Language Service Provider).
- 'Not much goes on and colleges do not have a good relationship with companies.' (North West of England, International Trade Manager, Chamber of Commerce).

The modes of training preferred by respondent companies are part-time evening (36.4%), part-time during working hours (26.6%), self-tuition (16%), intensive (12.7%) (see Figure 21). Evening classes are much criticised by respondent companies and International Trade Advisers as being more suitable for tourism than for business. In fairness, it should be recognised that adult education language provision is not designed for the individual needs of business learners.

Intensive language training is known to be 'effective' (though not miraculous) but proportionately more expensive. Successful self-tuition depends on the stamina and motivation of the individual. Part-time training during working hours has the advantages of being seen as a 'perk', benefiting from group motivation and being tailor-made for the company. In the East of England region there is support from the Regional Development Agency (EEDA) and a number of companies for a workable training formula which combines the positive attributes of semi-intensive, group study, business orientation and a combination of training in language and culture.

Which languages do European companies train in?

One of the major conclusions from the European data is that while English remains the most widely used language it is by no means the exclusive second language used for trading, while current levels of demand for English training are at the top of the table, other languages, such as Spanish, are coming to the fore. There is also demand for training in French, German and Italian. Russian and Japanese are the two non-EU languages which appear in the list of target languages for training, surprisingly. Training in Chinese is hardly evident at all.

English/Welsh, Scottish and Irish companies carry out mostly French and German language training in equal proportions. French is slightly ahead in England and Wales. In Poland we see the impact of Polish trade turning westward with a rise in demand for English. In Portugal, companies are making a considerable effort to improve their performance in languages, particularly English, but also German and French.

The share of English language training as a percentage of all training programmes undertaken per sample varies from the highest: Portugal (71%), Germany (61%) and France (60%), to the lowest: the Netherlands (30%) and Denmark (35%). Both these countries have such a significant advantage in English already, through its systematic inclusion in formal schooling from an early age, that it appears that less training is required by companies when employees join the workforce. German is clearly the second most targeted language for training in Poland (35%), Denmark (28%), the Netherlands (27%) and France (21%). The evidence suggests that most Europeans expect to operate in at least a trilingual environment: English is taken for granted and many learn another foreign language. In addition, they, of course, also have their native language. This often leaves monolingual Brits at a trading disadvantage, waiting for clients to speak English before communication can start.

Future training intentions

Future demand for training programmes follows the existing patterns with only minor differences. Somewhat paradoxically, training in English has slightly diminished with German achieving high demand, particularly in the countries which border Germany. The percentage of mentions for intended training in German is very high in Denmark and the Netherlands, where it is again on a par with English. The percentage of companies intending to undertake German training is also strong in Poland (31.6%) compared with 43.9% for English, which makes German second to English. There is a broad spread of proposed language training, with English language training predominant. Of the Portuguese companies responding to the REFLECT study, 43.9% intend to train in English and 31.6% in German, so the difference in demand is not excessively great. For other countries (e.g. Netherlands, England, Wales), Spanish is on the increase.

In the UK, 37% of English and Welsh companies, 12% in Northern Ireland and 38% in Scotland indicated that they intend to invest in future language training (see Figure 22). The planned pattern of language training is very similar to the current one, except that more companies plan to invest in Chinese, which reflects the rise in trade with China. In the Metra Martech study (1999), the number of companies proposing to train was lower, 27%. The majority of these (59%) were opting for German, due to the size of the German market. Fourteen percent were planning to undertake cultural briefings and the preferred cultures were East Asia (21%); Germany (18%), France (17%) and Spain (13%) (Metra Martech 1999: 30).

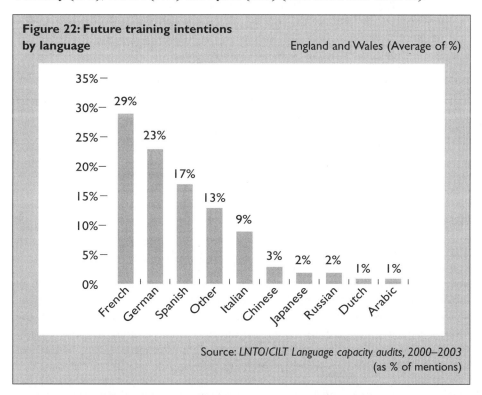

Figure 22: Future training intentions by language   England and Wales (Average of %)

Source: *LNTO/CILT Language capacity audits, 2000–2003*
(as % of mentions)

In the European countries participating in REFLECT a third to two-thirds of companies intend to undertake language training, which is higher than the percentage of training that has been undertaken in the past. The greatest potential growth for language training is in Spain (31%), followed by Sweden (25%), Portugal (21.7%), France (21%) and Poland (20%). English speaking countries come in the lower half: England and Wales, with an increase of 14%, Scotland, 16% and Ireland 17%.

Use of translators or interpreters

There are frequent references to the 'top four' languages, French, German, Spanish and Italian, but companies in the LNTO/CILT language skills audits also cite translation in a total of 29 languages, including Bulgarian, Turkish, Thai, Czech, Slovak, Latvian, Lithuanian, Korean, Maltese and Haitian. The range of different languages exemplifies the diversity of trading markets.

Translation and interpreting, along with language training, are the measures that require most high-level linguistic input. When asked whether they use translators or interpreters, an average of 51% of the companies surveyed replied in the affirmative. There were regional variations ranging from 43% of North East of England companies to 58% of North West of England.

One company does not like translation agencies as it would have to explain the confidential technicalities of its business, so it solves the problem by using its own linguists and then the services of its foreign clients who correct the texts. However, elsewhere in the sample, there is a general awareness that in certain situations there is a need to call upon a suitably experienced and qualified language professional.

Key points

The most persuasive argument about the importance of an international communication strategy comes from the British Chambers of Commerce language survey (2004) which identifies a direct correlation between the value an exporter places on language skills within his or her business and annual turnover. While the British Chambers of Commerce study does not investigate the international communication element within the export strategy, it acknowledges the integration of language skills and notes adaptation as a feature of the two most successful types of exporter, the Enablers and Adaptors.

The key to developing an international communication strategy in-company is more about changing the culture and achieving a level of recognition for the value of language and cultural skills, which in turn will lead to a set of actions. The LNTO/CILT language skills audits define and measure the elements of a strategy already in place in some companies, such as translating sales literature, employing native speakers, culturally adapting the website and investing in language training. Now the challenge is, through the spread of good practice, to spread such good practice to help move Opportunists through to the Developer phase, Developers through to the Adaptor phase and help Adaptors become Enablers. Growing awareness of the benefits that can accrue is known to lead to a more effective selection of tactics that eventually make up an effective international communication strategy.

five

Key recommendations

Focus of the chapter

On the surface, the findings from the LNTO/CILT audits and the British Chambers of Commerce or Metra Martech (Department of Trade and Industry) surveys make bleak reading. They suggest that UK international companies are generally underperforming in a number of areas when it comes to communicating with overseas customers. Yet, at the same time, there are also examples of significant achievement on the part of some companies, including SMEs, and very encouraging signs of success in policy initiatives, particularly in business support measures and in educational provision. It is worth taking stock of how, given the current situation facing many companies, examples of good practice in business and successful initiatives in education can create a climate for positive change. Examples deriving from the various studies in this book provide the basis for a series of recommendations.

What are the issues facing many UK Exporters?

The critical finding of all the studies is the high number of companies experiencing either linguistic or cultural barriers in their international communication. Broadly speaking, between four and five out of ten exporting companies trading in non-English speaking markets appear to have experienced language barriers; and one in five has experienced cultural barriers in (mainly) Japan, France, the Middle East and China.

Of greater concern is the percentage of companies which are aware of and admit to losing business as a result of these barriers: up to one in four. And where companies do have people with foreign language skills, they tend to be found in the management, rather than in the staff on the 'front line', such as receptionists or switchboard operators.

Where companies do have access to in-house language skills, levels of proficiency are not particularly encouraging. A majority of companies report that their proficiency is either at basic or intermediate level. The British Chambers of Commerce finding that 80% of English exporters cannot conduct business in a foreign language seems further to corroborate this. The additional British Chambers of Commerce finding that 63% of the exporters have no formal strategy to maintain, or instigate, trade with non-English speaking businesses, suggests that an *ad hoc* approach to overcoming language barriers is fairly widespread.

Where do the solutions lie?

There are three macro-issues where existing good practice could, if extended to the wider business and educational community, have a significant impact on the UK's capability to trade effectively across borders, namely:

- Overcoming barriers to trade
- Developing international communication strategies
- Matching provision to demand.

Overcoming barriers to trade

Issue: The percentages of companies facing different types of international communication barriers are very likely all to be underestimates. This means there is a significant loss of trading potential that can be addressed with intervention policies. There is a need for more language and business culture training, especially for markets which are still in the early stages of opening up, such as Eastern Europe and China to the East, and Brazil and Spanish-speaking Latin America, and even parts of the USA, to the West.

Recommendations

There is a need for awareness raising measures: because many companies are unaware of (i) the issues regarding language and culture in trade; (ii) where to go for advice and guidance; and (iii) existing schemes designed to help them, such as the Export Communications Review scheme (ECR) and Passport to Export.

A campaign will need to be pursued to win hearts and minds at policy level, including within the Chambers and other major national institutions. There is a need for an approach that emphasises the interconnectedness of different measures (e.g. school curriculum revision; Language Centre provision for adults and Higher Education students; increasing the number of UK students and employees on placements abroad; ECR and Passport to Export).

When companies recognise they have a problem, they need flexible, immediate referral systems; e.g. regional foreign language call centres and language centres offering 'instant' translation or 'gist translation' for quick responses. New quality procedures, a system of Office Standards, could be drawn up to address international communication and how to deal more effectively with overseas customers.

Training takes more time and resource than many smaller companies may have available, so it will be necessary to consider more liberal entry regulations into the UK for incoming specialists in whose languages there is a notable shortage. Categories of 'useful' personnel should include shortage areas for native speakers; e.g. speakers of Mandarin and Brazilian Portuguese.

Any system that brings more key native speakers from abroad into UK companies should be seen as positive. Examples are overseas student exchanges and placements, exchanges of employees across borders through chambers and other intermediaries, cross-border secondments between companies.

Companies cannot learn all the languages of their markets, so there is a need for more information on which intermediary languages can be used in third countries, such as German in Hungary, Russian in Bulgaria. Companies also need to know where English can comfortably be used (but see next point).

Companies are trading everywhere in English as it is a recognised lingua franca of international business. Companies need to know where it is more acceptable to use English (such as the Netherlands) and where not (such as France). There is a need to raise awareness of 'International English' which is free of UK-specific idioms and slang, simplified to facilitate ease of comprehension by native speakers of other languages, including 'non-English' English.

Many companies are not aware of the existence of the Export Communications Review Scheme and how an international communication strategy can benefit their company's effectiveness in export markets (see next section). Over 1000 UK export companies have now been through the ECR scheme. The scheme would benefit from promotion and in particular, dissemination of examples of good practice from companies using the scheme.

Developing international communication strategies

Issue: In a rapidly increasing global market, it is vital to embed greater awareness of the economic benefits of language skills as a means of expanding international trade. Success for many companies will depend on formulating an effective strategy. This can be achieved primarily through the adoption of a range of measures amounting to a company-wide international communication strategy.

Many companies are already undertaking a range of linguistic measures which they find effective, but awareness of the idea and processes of an integrated international communication strategy could clearly be improved. Currently, only 11% of the English and Welsh companies in the LNTO/CILT studies claim to have an international communication strategy. This requires more strategic thinking rather than taking ad hoc measures. For example, reliance on agents and translators is quite marked, and this is known to be an issue. Reliance on using just English with an agent may make a company vulnerable to deception.

Very few companies invest in language and culture training and rate it highly. Knowledge about how to use translators and interpreters to best effect is not widespread and companies may not, for example, always be up-to-date with the advantages and disadvantages of web-based translation systems.

The success of the ECR scheme is apparent from the feedback of participating companies. Too few are yet aware of the existence of the ECR scheme and its valuable contribution to UK exporters and Export Education in general.

Recommendations

There is a need to support companies in understanding the benefits, and limitations, of using machine and web-based translation tools; in helping companies to know how to deploy professional interpreters and/or translators to best effect; and how to plan for and evaluate the return on investment which may be represented by good quality, targeted language and cultural training.

Conversely, language professionals in all commercial fields would benefit from professional refreshment in latest techniques, tools, approaches, and emerging new business practices.

Language training providers need to look carefully at why so few companies opt for training; although it is understood that language training, as a sub-set of training of any description, has not traditionally been high on the list of investment priorities, especially for SMEs.

From the *British Chambers of Commerce language survey* (2004) it is apparent that the two groups of Adaptors and Enablers are the most likely to incorporate the elements of a communication strategy within their export plan. Both these groups provide important profiles of company-types which can be promoted as exemplars to other companies.

There is a need for an Export Communications Strategy promotional campaign with Chamber/RLNs/UKTI approval and marketing, focusing on the excellent results among companies who have used the scheme to date.

The ECR scheme should continue to disseminate its good practice throughout Europe (e.g. through the Protocol2 project) so that its framework becomes a European standard.

There is a need to see more 'peer-group' examples of best practice: for example the Languages for Export Award winners could be more widely promoted as best practice case studies, illustrating for others where and how a company has profited from its language investments.

Matching provision to demand

Issue: There is growing evidence of a demand for a greater diversity of languages in business. Language education providers might consider how to introduce more exotic languages, building on emerging good practice in a number of Specialist Language Colleges. Filling the shortfall in skill deficiencies in the short term has obliged companies to rely more heavily on native speakers. There has been a rapid falling-off in registration on advanced language courses.

In the medium to long term, educational provision will require radical revisions to the range, content and level of languages on offer. For educational policy makers, the recommendations arising from the LNTO/CILT language skills audits are about improving current provision in German, Spanish and Italian; widening provision in 'rarer' languages like Chinese, Japanese and Russian; raising proficiency levels and extending language learning to those who will be at lower staffing grades and operating in a wide range of sectors and job functions; and placing greater emphasis on appreciation of the business cultures which have been identified as presenting particular challenges for international trade (France, China, Japan, Middle East).

Recommendations

While recognising the important work being undertaken in Specialist Language Colleges and initiatives like the Languages Ladder it is important to extend this work in language provision to be more closely aligned to business needs, in terms of the range of languages required and the level of competence.

Consideration needs to be given as a matter of urgency to means of maintaining and increasing the number of linguists in the country competent to a higher level of operation such as that required by employers including the Foreign and Commonwealth Officer.

There should be greater emphasis on education in the languages which are documented as presenting barriers to international trade: e.g. French, German, Italian, Spanish, Japanese, and Chinese. School provision in the last four languages is still extremely limited. Where second, and particularly community, languages are being taught, such as Panjabi, Arabic, the link between these and potential trade should be encouraged.

There should be greater emphasis on business cultures and area studies pertinent to markets where barriers have been identified: e.g. Japan, France, China, Germany and the Middle East. The fact that France still scores highly in terms of occasioning language and cultural barriers for UK trading companies, despite the commitment to French in education provision, suggests that more could be done in the curriculum to provide insights into French business culture at school, college and university.

There will need to be an expansion in schools with an international ethos and diverse languages curriculum. This may involve the development of a new international curriculum to be available in schools and universities, modelled on institutions like Atlantic College, or the Anglo-European School, Ingatestone.

Greater determination should be brought into hiring more overseas teachers and lecturers to bring their language and culture into classrooms in the UK, possibly with the addition of financial incentives, and especially in rarer languages.

A closer link could be established between the local curriculum in schools and universities and regional trade patterns (national trade patterns in Wales, Scotland) e.g. more German in the north of the UK; more Dutch in the East of England.

The future

For many companies effective international communication is not the only factor in export success, but it is an indispensable element. The British Chambers of

Commerce finding that there is a direct correlation between the value an exporter places on language skills and their annual turnover suggests that language and culture can give companies that all-important competitive edge. Opportunists' export sales are declining by an average of £50,000 a year per exporter, while Enablers' exports are increasing by an average of £290,000 a year per exporter. In other words, good international communication can make the difference between making an average market entry or making a highly profitable one.

The systems to help make this happen are consolidating and fostering positive impact; they need continued support. At the national level, the infrastructures are mostly in place: the LNTO/CILT has provided the research, and with backing from the DfES, RDAs, UKTI and some LSCs, has put in place the RLNs; a 10-year National Languages Strategy for England is being implemented, under the watchful eye of Dr Lid King, appointed to the post of National Director for Languages. In 20 years' time new curriculum schemes such as the Primary School Languages Programme and Specialist Language Colleges will have a major impact on UK business's trading prospects.

Despite publication of compelling research evidence and the positive outlook for the future, the current message is still only getting through to certain segments of business and society. The need for a fundamental change of culture is essential. This calls for the inception of a new 'export culture' with international communication as its key feature. Such a culture change would require implementation of a national strategy on international communication for UK business, connecting together to joint purpose the major business organisations with curriculum planners, educational institutions and key national and regional agencies as partners in driving change.

appendix I

European survey data

Taken together, the three studies REFLECT, ELISE and ELUCIDATE (see Figure 23 below) provide data and findings with which to compare business communications in ten countries of Europe (Denmark, France, Germany, the Netherlands, Poland, Portugal, Republic of Ireland, Spain, Sweden and the UK).

Figure 23: European survey samples

Country/Region	Survey (year)	Population size
England and Wales	LNTO/CILT(2000–2003)	2,292
Ireland	REFLECT (2001)	233
Poland	REFLECT (2001)	166
Portugal	REFLECT (2001)	213
Denmark	ELISE (1999/2000)	52
Netherlands	ELISE (1999/2000)	92
Northern Ireland	ELISE (1999/2000)	50
Scotland	ELISE (1999/2000)	139
Sweden	ELISE (1999/2000)	44
France (Central)	ELUCIDATE (1996)	245
Germany (Southern)	ELUCIDATE (1996)	171
Spain (Western)	ELUCIDATE (1996)	124

The ELISE survey was carried out during 1999/2000 and the data in the study is based on findings from a sample of 452 small and medium-sized enterprises (with up to 500 people) across five countries – Denmark, Ireland (North and South), the Netherlands, Scotland and Sweden. It followed on from the ELUCIDATE (1999) study which surveyed SMEs in comparable regions of England and other European countries (i.e. France, Germany and Spain).

ELUCIDATE: The postal survey was completed in mid-1997 and involved mailing of a carefully designed, piloted and translated questionnaire to over 5,000 companies in four European countries. In total 963 replies were received from companies satisfying the selection criteria.

The main findings of REFLECT are also comparable with those of the ELUCIDATE and ELISE projects since the methodology and tools were similar. All the studies, the LNTO/CILT language skills audits, ELISE, ELUCIDATE and REFLECT, apply the definition of SME, current at the time, namely a company with up to 500 employees.

The Figures below present the main data from each of the European surveys.

Figure 24: Languages in use in other parts of Europe

England and Wales		Ireland		Poland	
(Average of %) (n=2,292)		(n=233)		(n=166)	
French	45%	French	35%	English	88%
German	36%	German	25%	German	78%
Spanish	22%	Spanish	13%	Russian	37%
Italian	12%	Italian	8%	French	18%
Dutch	5%	Japanese	4%	Italian	7%
Chinese	3%	Dutch	3%	Spanish	3%
Japanese	3%	Portuguese	2%	Czech	2%
Russian	2%	Russian	1%	Dutch	1%
Portuguese	2%			Swedish	1%
Arabic	2%			Hungarian	1%

Portugal		Denmark		Northern Ireland	
(n=213)		(n=52)		(n=50)	
English	91%	English	92%	French	44%
French	79%	German	81%	German	26%
Spanish	54%	French	33%	Spanish	12%
German	23%	Swedish	19%	Dutch	4%
Italian	19%	Spanish	17%	Korean	4%
Swedish	1%	Norwegian	12%		
Dutch	0.5%	Italian	6%		
Norwegian	0.5%	Portuguese	4%		
Russian	0.5%				
Danish	0.5%				
Greek	0.5%				

Netherlands		Scotland		Sweden	
(n=92)		(n=139)		(n=44)	
English	82%	French	43%	English	86%
German	82%	German	42%	German	25%
French	53%	Spanish	17%	French	14%
Spanish	15%	Italian	14%		
Italian	7%	Japanese	10%		
		Chinese	4%		
		Swedish	4%		
		Russian	4%		

France		Germany		Spain	
(n=245)		(n=171)		(n=124)	
English	83%	English	93%	English	77%
German	44%	French	54%	French	57%
Spanish	42%	Italian	32%	German	20%
Italian	17%	Spanish	18%	Portuguese	14%
Chinese	2%	Czech	4%	Italian	13%
Portuguese	2%	Russian	2%		
Dutch	2%	Croatian	2%		
Russian	2%				
Japanese	<1%				
Arabic	<1%				
Czech	<1%				

Source: ELUCIDATE, ELISE and REFLECT data
(as % of sample)

Figure 25: Levels of competence

Level of competence	England & Wales	Ireland	Poland	Portugal	France	Germany	Spain
	(n= Average of %)	(n=147)	(n=732)	(n=418)	(n=295)	(n=187)	(n=154)
Basic	37%	29%	25%	32%	34%	21%	11%
Intermediate	16%	12%	44%	20%	15%	28%	40%
Advanced	15%	13%	28%	46%	26%	25%	41%
Fluent	22%	38%	3%	0.2%	19%	12%	3%
Bilingual	10%	8%	0.5%	2%	6%	14%	5%

(as % of mentions)
NB This question was not asked for ELISE

Figure 26: Cultures/regions where cultural barriers are particularly evident

England and Wales		Ireland		Poland	
(Average of %)		(n=30)		(n=12)	
Japan	16%	Japan	23%	Germany	33%
France	12%	France	20%	France	17%
Middle East	12%	Germany	20%	Italy	17%
China	11%	China	7%		
Germany	9%				
Italy	6%				
Spain	5%				
SEA	4%				

Portugal		Denmark		Northern Ireland	
(n=34)		(n=52)		(n=50)	
Japan	15%	England	92%	France	44%
UK	12%	Germany	81%	Germany	26%
Brazil	12%	France	33%	Spain	12%
Africa	12%	Sweden	19%	Netherlands	4%
Korea	9%	Spain	17%	Korea	4%
		Norway	12%		
		Italy	6%		
		Portugal	4%		

Netherlands		Scotland		Sweden	
(n=92)		(n=139)		(n=44)	
England	82%	France	43%	England	86%
Germany	82%	Germany	42%	Germany	25%
France	53%	Spain	17%	France	14%
Spain	15%	Italy	14%		
Italy	7%	Japan	10%		
		China	4%		
		Sweden	4%		
		Russia	4%		

Germany		Spain		France	
(n=16)		(n=27)		(n=29)	
Japan	31%	France	26%	Japan	17%
Italy	13%	Germany	15%	Germany	14%
		Africa	11%	Middle East	10%
		UK	7%	Far East	10%

(as % of mentions)

Figure 27: Comments on causes of cultural barriers

Country	Quotation
Africa	• Polygamy, though illegal, is common. This plus other cultural differences impacted proposals and products.
China	• Colour – red on our promotion. • Takes a considerable effort to acquire understanding of etiquette.
France	• Conservative negotiating stance. • From a sales perspective needs direct on the ground support. • Lack of language skills plus cultural knowledge of the selling process.
Germany	• Etiquette and way of addressing people.
India	• Often business done at home, thus need understanding of Indian business life. Puts you at ease – falsely.
Iran	• Difficult to convince in daily work.
Ireland	• More laid-back approach. Not punctual.
Japan	• Almost impenetrable because of cultural approach.
Korea	• Difficult to understand who to speak to – they have a hierarchy which is very important.
Middle East	• Time keeping/observing meeting arrangements. • Prefer to be dealt with by a male/lack of respect for women in junior roles. • Work weekends but not Thursdays.
Netherlands	• Efficient but very cautious. • Very precise. Want perfection.
Saudi Arabia	• Problems for female sales staff – we used males as this circumvented difficulties.
Spain	• Relaxed attitude/lack of attention to detail. • Negotiating often with 4–8 people ... to confuse.
Turkey	• Prefer to be dealt with by a male/lack of respect for women in junior roles. • Work weekends but not Thursdays.
USA	• Different psyche. • USA business etiquette more formal than UK. • Time and employment matters.

Source: ELISE (1997)

appendix 2

Glossary of common abbreviations

BLIS Professionals | A database of language experts for business (translators, interpreters, language trainers, cultural consultancy)

DfES | Department for Education and Skills

DTI | Department of Trade and Industry

ECR | Export Communications Review (managed by the British Chambers of Commerce)

ELISE | European Language and International Strategy Development in SMEs, a project partially funded by the EU Leonardo da Vinci programme

ELUCIDATE | European Language an Culture Development and Training, an EU Leonardo Project, published as *Business communication across borders: A study of language use and practice in European companies* (Hagen 1999)

EU | European Union

LNTO | Languages National Training Organisation, now part of CILT, the National Centre for Languages

REFLECT | Review of Foreign Language and Culture Training Needs (an EU Leonardo supported project; see Hagen and Salomao 2003)

SLC | Specialist Language College

SME | Small to medium-sized enterprise (defined as up to 500 employees in this study)

TPUK | Trade Partners UK, now incorporated within UKTI

UKTI | UK Trade and Investment (successor to Trade Partners UK and DTI)

references

ACCAC (1999) *Report of survey of employers' needs for bilingual competence*. ACCAC (Qualifications, Curriculum and Assessment Authority for Wales).

British Chambers of Commerce (2003–2004) *The British Chambers of Commerce language survey*, The Impact of Foreign Languages on British Business, *Part 1: The Qualitative results* (2003); *Part 2: The Quantitative survey* (2004). London: British Chambers of Commerce.

DfES (2002) *Languages for all: Languages for life*. DfES Publications.

ELISE (2001) *European language and international strategy development in SMEs* (co-funded by the Leonardo da Vinci programme). **www.interesourcegroup.com/elise**.

ELUCIDATE (1999) published as Hagen, S. (ed). **www.interact.int.com/elucidate**.

Eurobaromètre 54 Special Report (2001) *Les Européens et les langues*. INRA (EUROPE).

FLAIR-EUROPE: A LINGUA project report, published as Hagen, S. (1993).

Gesteland, R. R. (2003) *Cross-cultural business behaviour*. Copenhagen: Copenhagen Business School Press.

Hagen, S. and Salomao, R. (2003) *Estrategias de comunicacao das empresas exportadoras*. Lisbon: Universidade Aberta.

Hagen, S. (ed) (1999) *Business communication across borders: A study of language use and practice in European companies*. CILT.

Hagen, S. (1998) (a video training pack development supported by the Leonardo da Vinci programme). InterAct International.

Hagen, S. (ed) (1993) *Languages in European business: a regional survey of small and medium sized companies*. CILT.

Hoffman, R. C. and Gopinath, C. (1994) 'The importance of international business to the strategic agenda of US CEOs'. *Journal of International Business Studies*, Third Quarter: 625–637.

INTERCOMM (2002-2004) *International communication skills for enhanced mobility and trade* (a Leonardo da Vinci funded project). **www.intercommproject.com**.

Kedia, B. L. and Daniel, S. J. (2003) *U.S. business needs for employees with international expertise*. A paper prepared for the Needs for Global Challenges Conference at Duke University.

LNTO/CILT *Language skills capacity audits* (2000–2003). (Principal investigator and demand-side author: Hagen, S.). LNTO/CILT:
• East of England language skills capacity audit 2003
• Wales language skills capacity audit 2002
• Language skills and strategies in the North West 2002
• South West region of England language skills capacity audit 2001
• Yorkshire and Humber language skills capacity audit 2001
• West Midlands language skills capacity audit 2001
• North East language skills capacity audit 2000

Metra Martech (1997) *DTI language study*. Unpublished research report prepared for the Department of Trade and Industry.

Metra Martech (1999) *DTI language study*. Unpublished research report prepared for the Department of Trade and Industry.

Moxon, R., O'Shea, E., Brown, M. and Escher, C. (1997) *Changing US business needs for international expertise*. Center for International Business Education and Research (CIBER), University of Washington Business School.

National Languages Strategy (2002) see DfES (2002).

Nuffield Foundation (2000) *Languages, the next generation: the final report of the Nuffield Languages Inquiry*. The Nuffield Foundation.

PROTOCOL 2 (2002-2004), *Programme and materials for the training of language and communication auditors of European SMEs* (a Leonardo da Vinci funded project). **www.protocol2.info**.

REFLECT (2002) *Review of foreign language and cultural training needs* (a Leonardo da Vinci funded project). **www.reflectproject.com** (see also Hagen, S. and Salomao, R., 2003).

Tomlinson, M. (2004) 14–19 Curriculum and qualifications reform: Final report of the Working Group on 14–19 reform. DfES.

Tung, R. L., (1996) 'Managing in Asia: cross-cultural dimensions'. In: *Managing across cultures issues and perspectives*, Joynt, P. & M. Warner (eds) London: International Thomson Business Press, 1996.

UKTI's Passport to Export Scheme. **www.uktradeinvest.gov.uk**.

Webb, M. S., Mayer, K. R., Pioche, V. and Allen, L. C. (1999) Internationalization of American Business Education. *Management International Review*, 39: 379–397.

Further information

BLIS Professionals: **www.blis.org.uk/professionals**

British Chambers of Commerce: **www.chamberonline.co.uk**

Interpreting for the public services: a guide to commissioning excellent interpreting services. **www.cilt.org.uk/publications/online.htm#psi**

Language training in the engineering industry: e-mail publications@cilt.org.uk.

Languages Work provides inspiration, advice, activities and links that help to show the true value of language through resources and a website: **www.languageswork. org.uk**

Regional Language Networks: **www.cilt.org.uk/rln**

Translation – getting it right: a guide to buying translations: e-mail: publications@cilt. org.uk